FINDING

→·YOUR·←

FOCUS

FINDING

→YOUR←

FOCUS

JUDITH GREENBAUM, PH.D.
AND GERALDINE MARKEL, PH.D.

McGraw·Hill

New York   Chicago   San Francisco   Lisbon   London   Madrid   Mexico City
Milan   New Delhi   San Juan   Seoul   Singapore   Sydney   Toronto

Library of Congress Cataloging-in-Publication Data

Greenbaum, Judith.
      Finding your focus : practical strategies for the everyday challenges facing adults
with ADD / Judith Greenbaum and Geraldine Markel.
            p.   cm.
      ISBN 0-07-145396-2 (alk. paper)
      1. Attention-deficit disorder in adults—Popular works.   I. Markel, Geraldine
Ponte, 1939–   II. Title.

RC394.A85G74   2005
616.85′89—dc22   2005007345

5 6 7 8 9 0   DOC/DOC   0 9

ISBN 0-07-145396-2

McGraw-Hill books are available at special quantity discounts to use as premiums and
sales promotions, or for use in corporate training programs. For more information, please
write to the Director of Special Sales, Professional Publishing, McGraw-Hill, Two Penn
Plaza, New York, NY 10121-2298. Or contact your local bookstore.

This book is printed on acid-free paper.

Dedicated to Stephen I. Markel

1966–2004

Contents

PART II

Practical Strategies for Everyday Problems

PART III

Looking Ahead to the Future

Acknowledgments

WE WOULD LIKE to express our gratitude to our colleagues and friends in the field of ADD: Russell Barkley, Wilma Fellman, Ned Hallowell, Thom Hartmann, Terry Matlen, Kathleen Nadeau, Harvey Parker, Patricia Quinn, John Ratey, Arthur Robin, Larry Silver, Sari Solden, and Lynn Weiss. These physicians, researchers, therapists, and educators have led the way toward a new understanding of adults with ADD and have helped countless adults in the process.

We would also like to pay our respects to CHADD (Children and Adults with Attention Deficit Disorder) and ADDA (Attention Deficit Disorder Association), two national organizations dedicated to providing adults with ADD with the latest research and information to help them survive and thrive.

And finally, a salute to our clients of the past twenty-five years, who continue to strive to make a better life for themselves.

Introduction

WE WROTE THIS BOOK to help bring greater order and hope to adults with ADD. We have seen how even one small improvement in focusing one's attention or organizing one's life can begin a powerful process of greater self-management and productivity. Although our book specifically addresses people with ADD, it is really for anyone who has problems with distractibility and disorganization.

We see *Finding Your Focus* as a complement to several excellent books on the market, namely Hallowell and Ratey's *Driven to Distraction* and *Delivered from Distraction* and Solden's *Women with Attention Deficit Disorder* and *Journeys Through ADDulthood*. (The Resources section at the end of the book provides more information on these and other recommended references.) These books and others like them were written to help adults with ADD understand, accept, and live with their condition. Building on this foundation, our book outlines specific strategies, checklists, and routines for daily living.

Finding Your Focus draws on current research and employs our own clinical experience to help you develop solutions to some of the most important issues and problems you are facing at home and at work.

You will find specific strategies to solve the unique challenges of ADD. We provide routines you can adopt to make these new strategies become habits; checklists to assist you in managing your time and organizing your life; and ways to talk to yourself to help you manage attention problems, distractibility, and impulsivity. We encourage you to adapt our tools, strategies, routines, and checklists to your personality and lifestyle and to use your creativity to invent strategies of your own.

You can begin working on any problem in the book, but if you do skip around, please be sure to read Chapter 3 first, as it describes the tools you will use in working on the problems discussed in subsequent chapters.

Using the practical tips and strategies in our book can help you reach the following goals:

- Fulfill your daily responsibilities in new, more effective ways.
- Bypass and overcome the symptoms of ADD that interfere with a satisfying life.
- Enhance your performance at home and at work and further develop your potential.

In Chapter 1, you'll find information on the causes and major symptoms of ADD, the different types of attention, and three important tips for dealing with ADD. In Chapter 2, we provide checklists so you can identify your strengths and difficulties, as well as helpful and difficult environments in which to work. Tips to help use your strengths to bypass weaknesses are included, with steps to move from self-awareness to self-improvement. Chapter 3, as we mentioned earlier, is one you don't want to skip. Here we give you the research-based tools (including self-talk, visualizing, routines, and checklists) to use throughout the rest of the book to help you focus on and solve various problems you may have at home or at work.

Chapters 4 through 8 are devoted to specific problems and ways to solve them and prevent them from overtaking your life. In Chapter 4, we explain why people with ADD often lose things, and we outline routines to help you find your keys, glasses, car, and similar items. Chapter 5 helps you decide when clutter is a problem and features tips and steps to help you clean up your room, attack a pile of papers, organize your kitchen, and maintain a relatively neat home. Chapter 6 explains ways in which poor time management can cause serious problems both at home and at work and includes issues such as perfectionism. You'll find techniques (such as creating daily "to do" lists and monthly calendars) to enhance time management; strategies and checklists for completing complex tasks (such as writing grant proposals) in a timely manner; and routines for getting to work or appointments on time. Chapter 7 describes the ways procrastination can interfere with daily life and lists specific tips to overcome procrastination. You'll learn how to pay bills on time and how to organize complex tasks such as preparing for a trip, throwing a party, or giving a presentation at work. Chapter 8 is especially important because it delves into the sensitive issue of why a person with ADD may irritate others inadvertently. We reveal the reasons for this problem and provide strategies to improve relationships. Tips and checklists address how to read cues from others, talk less, and listen better. We also suggest ways to renegotiate relationships and follow through on commitments.

In Chapter 9, we give you information on an important decision you may be facing: whether to try medication for ADD. To help you decide, we list the types and effects of various medications; we provide checklists to help you monitor the positive and negative effects of medication; and we offer routines to help prevent you from misplacing your medication.

The last chapter, Chapter 10, addresses the difficult issues involved in making decisions and setting goals. To overcome these obstacles, we offer a variety of checklists, diagrams, and visual aids to help you solve problems, make decisions, and set realistic and relevant goals.

It is important to understand that this is not an all-or-nothing book. You should feel no guilt for not wanting or not being able to utilize all the strategies provided. Rather, we suggest that you work toward as many or as few changes as you wish—just be sure to do them one at a time. It is our hope that once you start implementing our strategies, you will begin to move from an unsatisfactory life to one bright with promise.

FINDING

→YOUR←

FOCUS

PART I

———

Getting to Know Yourself

1

Understanding ADD

ADD IS IN THE NEWS almost daily. Questions such as "Isn't ADD just a cop-out for someone who is lazy?" or "We all have problems with attention at one time or another—so, what's the big deal?" or "Is there really such a thing as ADD?" are bandied about on talk shows, in newspapers, and at cocktail parties.

The answer to the last question is yes, there is such a thing as ADD. It's not just a cop-out for anyone who is lazy. In fact, people with ADD often work harder than anyone else to meet their responsibilities at home and at work. Although there is no blood test for ADD (as is also true for bipolar disorder or obsessive-compulsive disorder), you can find out whether you have it through careful neuropsychological evaluation.

ADD is considered a neurological disorder, and recent research on the brain has identified regions in the prefrontal cortex that are smaller or less active than normal in people with ADD. There is also a tendency for ADD to be genetic. In fact, you may have discovered your ADD after your son or daughter was diagnosed with it in school.

It is estimated that about 4 percent of the adult population of the United States, or 8 million people, have ADD. So, you are not the only one in the world who is distracted and/or disorganized! In addition, a large proportion of the rest of us have had problems with attention and organization at one time or another. Some of these problems are due to the crazy world in which we live, which demands so much of us. Often we are trying to do two (or more) things at once (such as trying to be the best parents we can be while doing more than what's required of us at work). We have even coined a new word for this: *multitasking*. However, the more we try to multitask, the more we will have problems with attention: focusing it, sustaining it, and screening out distractions. If you have ADD, you may think you can multitask successfully, but it is essentially impossible.

In addition, the older we get, the more difficulty we have focusing our attention. This begins to happen in our forties (about the same time we begin to need glasses for reading). Problems with attention and organization are not unique to people with ADD, but if you have ADD, these problems will be greater in intensity and can seriously interfere with your life. Many people with ADD are underemployed or unemployed, or frequently change jobs. They are more likely to suffer from stress and depression, have low aspirations for themselves, and often feel "dumb."

It's important to understand that having ADD does not make you any less smart than other people. Most people with ADD have at least average intelligence, and others are even gifted. However, it is often the tasks of daily living that can trip you up.

For example, Hannah, an accomplished painter, totaled her last car because she forgot to check the oil and the engine seized up (she also forgot to renew her driver's license). Dwight, a respected teacher, keeps losing money because it often falls out of his pocket, in which he shoves it without thinking. Dan, a plant manager, can't find his keys in the morning. Milly, who operates her own business, can't find her car. The stories from our coaching sessions are endless.

Recognizing Symptoms

Most of the world tends to think that having ADD means having problems with attention and distractibility, period. However, if you have

ADD, you may also experience many subtle problems of which you might not be aware. These include the following:

- Acting or speaking impulsively, without thinking
- Difficulty making decisions
- Restlessness
- Difficulty solving problems and thinking clearly
- Disorganization at work and at home
- Frequently losing things
- Poor sense of time
- Easily becoming frustrated or angered
- Difficulty following rules or waiting in line
- Difficulty keeping a job
- Difficulty keeping friends
- Alcoholism and drug abuse

As if this were not enough, people with ADD often develop emotional problems due to their history of school failure and/or under-achievement. Add to that the frustration and anxiety that can come with constantly trying to be successful in a world that seems to often misunderstand you and not give you enough time to think things through. The good news is that nobody has *all* of these problems, or even most of them!

You need to understand which problems you do have, and when and in what situations they occur. Often problems with attention are situation specific. For example, you may have difficulty paying attention when you are bored, but, boy, when you are doing something that interests you, you can work on it for hours.

Many of us have problems with attention or organization. Does this mean we have ADD? Not necessarily. Unless these problems greatly interfere with your life, you probably don't have ADD.

Getting a Diagnosis: How to Tell If You Have ADD

Evaluations for ADD usually begin with a checklist in which you examine all the symptoms you may be having. If your physician doesn't have such a checklist, go to a licensed psychologist or social worker who specializes in ADD. If the answers on the checklist point to ADD, you may want to go one step further. An in-depth neuropsychological evaluation can uncover what your specific difficulties are—whether you have problems with working memory, or you process information slowly, or you have dyslexia. This type of evaluation can give you a good picture of yourself—highlighting your strengths and your weaknesses. ADD can make you feel confused and frustrated because your troubles do not make sense to you. For example, you feel in your bones that you're smart, but you're not making the grade. Often it is only with a comprehensive evaluation that the subtle yet complex problems underlying these difficulties can be isolated.

In addition, you may want an official diagnosis of ADD in order to become eligible for support and accommodations under the Americans with Disabilities Act (ADA). Accommodations in the workplace can help you maximize your strengths while bypassing your weaknesses. Here are some examples of accommodations:

- Arranging for you to have a distraction-free workstation
- Requiring you to read less
- Providing you with someone to take notes while you talk
- Having someone help you organize your office

ADD Is Not the Only Cause of Attention Problems

Another reason for getting a diagnosis is that there could be many causes for your having problems focusing your attention that have little to do with ADD. Here are some possibilities:

- A noisy and chaotic environment
- Work that is too difficult for you and not the right fit for your skills (If you continue to be faced with this task and you don't receive any help, your mind will eventually begin to wander.)
- Work that is boring and/or repetitive (Here too it is hard to keep your mind on the work.)
- Chronic stress that makes it difficult for you to concentrate

- Perfectionism (You think that nothing you do is ever good enough, so you work and rework something—often missing deadlines. Perfectionism can lead to procrastination in some people with ADD, but it is also a common trait among many other people.)
- Anxiety or depression that interferes with your ability to concentrate
- Learning disabilities or dyslexia—without ADD—which can cause you to have such difficulty reading that you eventually stop paying attention when you are reading
- Side effects of certain medications that can make it difficult to concentrate
- Psychiatric or seizure disorders

In order to determine if your attention problems are caused by ADD or are related to something else, you should consult with a physician, psychologist, or psychiatrist. It is often difficult to determine which problems are caused by depression, anxiety, or a physical ailment such as diabetes, and which are caused by ADD.

Some Treatment Options

There are essentially three approaches to treating ADD:

- Counseling with a psychiatrist, psychologist, or social worker
- Medication
- Coaching or retraining

Psychotherapy can help you understand ADD, how it affects you, and how to come to terms with it. It can address such conditions as anxiety, depression, and feelings of failure that may be either separate from ADD or caused by it.

We're coaches, so we're a little biased here, but coaching and retraining can provide you with strategies you can use in your daily life to prevent or find a way around your particular problem. A coach can also provide you with the encouragement to get back on track. This book contains the many strategies we have used for more than thirty years in treating our clients with ADD.

While taking medications for ADD can allow you to profit from coaching and retraining, medication alone is rarely enough to get you back on track. We talk more about the decision to take medication in Chapter 9.

Many people with ADD combine all three approaches for the best results.

The Role of Attention

Attention is the key to effective functioning. It is also the cornerstone of memory. If you don't or can't pay attention to a piece of new information, you will not be able to remember it or use it. If you don't pay attention to directions, you will not be able to correctly finish a task or solve a problem. If you don't pay attention to where you are putting something, you probably won't be able to find it when you want it.

We are not defining *attention* as passively glancing over a passage to be read or letting something "go in one ear and out the other." Many of us think we are paying attention when we behave this way, but in fact, we are not. Rather, attention is an active process. It involves consciously focusing on new information long enough to incorporate it into your working memory. Researchers tend to agree that there are four types of attention:

- *Selective attention* helps us single out one important thing on which to focus and at the same time screen out unrelated or unimportant things.
- *Sustained attention* helps us maintain our focus until we complete a task.
- *Shifting attention* enables us to move smoothly from one selected thing to another and back, as needed.
- *Divided attention* enables us to attend to more than one thing at a time.

If you have ADD, you may have trouble with one or more aspects of attention. For example, you can have difficulty in both focusing your attention and in deciding what aspect of a situation to focus on (and what to screen out). Screening out distractions can be difficult for people with ADD. These distractions can be audio (such as other people talking or a bird singing) or visual (such as an accident on the highway or too many posters and notices on the wall of your office).

In addition, thoughts and emotions can be distractions. For example, if you are trying to solve a problem when you are worried or depressed, you will have difficulty focusing on what you are doing. It can be equally distracting if you are thinking of the vacation you are planning to take next week while trying to complete a project.

Sustaining attention can be a problem for anyone who is working on a boring task. Most of us have to invent a few tricks in order keep ourselves working on something that doesn't interest us. However, with ADD, you often turn away from boring tasks and even have considerable difficulty finishing a task about which you were initially enthusiastic. Shifting attention back and forth among several tasks can also be difficult because the need to shift attention just compounds the problems you have in focusing your attention in the first place.

Divided attention is the most problematic. For example, it is relatively easy to talk on the telephone while washing the dishes. However, it is relatively impossible to listen to someone talk and to read at the same time — if we want to get something out of either activity. A requirement to work on several projects simultaneously, shifting from task to task and back, is a recipe for failure when you have ADD.

ADD and Organizational Abilities

ADD can affect both your attention and your organizational abilities. These organizational abilities are called *executive functions*. Executive functions are a group of coordinated skills that help us see a task through from beginning to end. In many cases, the most serious problems people have both at home and at work are caused by faults in executive functioning.

To understand executive functions in action, think of an executive of a large corporation, working in his wood-paneled corner office high on the sixtieth floor. He is on the telephone. His secretary stands by his side, handing him letters to sign while his second-in-command waits impatiently in the outer office with an important contract to discuss. Think of all the things this executive has to do in order to make his company run smoothly:

- Set production goals for the company
- Make plans for both the long term and short term
- Monitor the company's progress
- Conduct top-level meetings
- Make decisions affecting every part of the company
- Analyze a potential project to see what is required
- Develop policies and procedures
- Prioritize work to be done
- Set time lines for projects
- Change course if necessary
- Look back when a job is completed to determine what went right—or wrong

He does all of this while conducting a telephone conversation, talking to individual staff members, and dictating and signing letters.

Not everyone can do all of this. There is a huge range of abilities when it comes to executive functions. Fortunately, most of us do not need all or most of these abilities in order to function well in our daily lives. But, if you think about it, we do need to be able to do many of these things. Good executive functioning is important for work, the tasks of daily living, and family/social life. Executive functions help us perform the following tasks:

- Get to work on time (and get to appointments on time)
- Begin and complete an important project in a timely fashion
- Manage money (and stop impulsive spending)
- Solve problems effectively and efficiently—weighing all alternatives

- Use good judgment (and not act impulsively)
- Overcome procrastination
- Interact appropriately with other people
- Remember where we've put things
- Organize our household or office

Throughout this book, you will find strategies to help you with these executive functions.

Is There an Upside to Having ADD?

Although people with ADD may have problems with attention, time management, and organization, they can be very creative. Your daydreaming and "stream of consciousness" thinking can pay off in the form of new inventions, beautiful art, and novel solutions to sticky problems. You can often think "outside of the box" and can serve as an "idea" person on a team working on a new product.

With ADD, you can often see the "big picture"—what something will look like once it is accomplished. This is important when you're working on a new project or inventing a new product. Conversely, you may often notice details that others don't see: a small glitch in a plan or something out of place that must be rectified before progress can continue.

In addition, you can be a lot of fun to be around because you can be spontaneous and often have novel ways of entertaining yourself and other people. Some people with ADD have an uncanny ability to *hyperfocus* on subjects they find interesting, to the exclusion of everything else. This ability can be very useful, depending on what you are supposed to be doing at the moment. In addition, you may possess many fine traits that have nothing to do with ADD. *Remember, ADD does not define who you are.*

How This Book Can Help You

We hope that this chapter has helped you understand more about ADD. As you read the next chapter, you will come to understand that ADD is only a part of who you are. It is important that you accept the fact that you have ADD and view it as a challenge to overcome.

In succeeding chapters, you will learn how to manage your attention and use newly acquired time-management and organizational skills as you go through the tasks of daily living. Just by practicing the following three basic strategies, you will gain a greater sense of control over your life: Use routines to help you locate some of the things that are important to you—such as your keys and your wallet (Chapter 4); this will enable you to save yourself a great deal of time. Get into the habit of writing daily "to do" lists (Chapter 6); this will help you organize your day, and you will be able to accomplish much more—in less time! Learn how to make a plan to help you bring in your next big project at work on time; this will give you a great feeling of accomplishment, and maybe a raise.

In this book, we show you how to accomplish these important tasks as well as many others to help you find your focus and get on the right track!

2

Identifying Your Strengths and Weaknesses

YOU CAN BECOME VERY confused about yourself when you have ADD. Sometimes you may feel kind of dumb, and at other times you know you are as smart as the next guy, even smarter. Unfortunately, many people with ADD forget their smart side and focus only on the "dumb" things they do. In actuality, they don't do "dumb" things; rather, they have glitches or weaknesses that often trip them up. Would you call a near-sighted person "dumb" because he or she can't see well enough to read a street sign? Well, a person with ADD is not stupid just because he or she has problems with attention or organization. You can be very smart—even gifted—and still have ADD.

In Chapter 1, we discussed the fact that people with ADD have strengths as well as weaknesses. They can be exceptionally creative. They are "idea" people and often have interesting (and offbeat) suggestions to contribute to problem-solving efforts. They can be friendly and outgoing. People with ADD have individual strengths that they often don't even recognize because they are so wrapped up with what they can't do.

In our coaching sessions, we have seen many people with ADD who have low self-esteem. Because they have been criticized so many times, by friends, family, and coworkers, they don't think of themselves as smart or capable. They tend to underrate their natural talents or gifts. Often they are underemployed because they don't even dare to aspire to the things they are capable of doing—or the things they want to do.

If you have ADD, you need to become as aware of your strengths as you are of your weaknesses. Your strengths can help you correct or bypass your weaknesses. It is on your strengths that you will build a good career and a good life. You have to keep reminding yourself to take pride in the things you do well and easily, even as you try to improve on some of your problem areas.

Research underscores the importance of getting to know yourself as a first step toward self-improvement. Getting to know yourself, or self-awareness, means understanding both your strengths and your weaknesses. A better understanding of your profile of strengths, weaknesses, and interests will help you manage your ADD.

Unfortunately, self-awareness is not a strong suit of people with ADD—largely because of their problems with attention and distractibility. In order to become self-aware, it is necessary for you to consciously focus your attention on what you are doing, not all of the time but a large part of the time.

Identifying Your Strengths

Take some time to list your strengths: the activities or tasks that you do easily and well. When you find your areas of strength, the next step will be to understand how and when these strengths can help you bypass or correct your weaknesses.

In Table 2.1, we have listed some common talents and abilities to get you started on your way toward learning about your own strengths. There are many more that are not on this list. Put a check next to the types of activities that you do well or most easily, and try to write an example next to each item you have checked.

Table 2.1 Self-Check: What I Do Well

Talents/Activities	Examples
Building things	
Fixing things	
Reading	
Writing	
Observing/noticing details	
Getting the big picture	
Using/developing graphs or diagrams	
Understanding/empathizing with people	
Drawing/designing	
Math	
Science	
Problem solving	
Inventing	
Working with computers	
Teaching/explaining	
Knowledge of current affairs/politics	
Setting goals	
Working quickly	
Working accurately	

continued

Table 2.1 continued

Staying on track until finished

Following through on promises

Being on time

Foreseeing possible problems

Making decisions

Asking for help

Abilities/Attributes	Examples
Enthusiastic	
Motivated	
Hardworking	
Creative	
Friendly/outgoing	
Leading/directing	
Funny/entertaining	
Calm	
Good memory	
Good organizational skills	
Smart/intelligent	
Intuitive	
Other	

Keep adding to this list from time to time as you think of other things you do well. If you are really down on yourself, you can post this list on your refrigerator so that you can glance at it regularly. Also, try to end each day thinking about something you did that day that pleased you or made you proud. (Remember that you can be proud of making progress toward a goal as well as actually achieving it.)

Understanding Your Weaknesses

In addition to identifying your strengths, it is equally important for you to start examining the weaknesses and glitches caused by ADD and understand when they interfere with what you are trying to do. In Table 2.2, check all the difficulties that apply to you, and try to write an example next to each one.

You can add to this list from time to time, as you become aware of other specific difficulties you might have that are related to ADD.

Distinguishing Between Helpful and Difficult Environments

People with ADD need to live and work in environments that help keep their attention focused, help them work steadily on a task until it is completed, and help them stay as organized as possible. Some environments hinder rather than help us perform well. In getting to know yourself further, it is important to identify environments and conditions that help you perform with comfort, speed, and accuracy. It is equally important to identify environments and conditions that interfere with your performance.

In Table 2.3, read each of the descriptions, and put a plus or minus to indicate whether the environment (or condition) helps or hinders your performance. Then, provide an example if one comes to mind.

Table 2.2 Self-Check: What I Have Trouble With

Difficulties	Examples
My attention keeps wandering.	
I'm very disorganized.	
I keep losing things.	
I get lost easily.	
I'm often late for appointments.	
I rarely pay my bills on time.	
I often forget to renew my driver's license.	
I have too much to do.	
I have a hard time completing many of the things I have to do.	
I have a hard time getting started.	
My home (or office) is a pigsty, cluttered and messy.	
People tell me I don't listen to them.	
Sometimes I blurt out things for which I'm sorry later.	
I have difficulty keeping a job.	
I get overwhelmed when I have to make a presentation at work.	
I have a hard time making up my mind.	
Other	

Identifying Strategies That Work for You

Another part of self-awareness is becoming aware of the many strategies we already use that help us overcome some of the problems associated with ADD. Many people with ADD have learned to adapt by developing strategies that help them work relatively effectively and efficiently. Here are some examples from our clients:

- "I place a ruler under each line I read to make sure I don't skip a word or lose my place."
- "I write an aisle-by-aisle shopping list for myself before I go to the supermarket."
- "When someone gives me a phone number, I read it back to him or her to be sure I've got it right."
- "I always give myself extra time to get someplace."
- "I bought one of those project boxes to help me organize my desk."

You can develop your own repertoire of strategies by examining those that have previously worked for you. Doing this will enable you to figure out other situations in which those strategies will work.

Self-Monitoring

Self-monitoring is a good strategy to use to increase your awareness of both your effective and problematic behaviors. If you want to improve a skill or break a habit, then you need to monitor when and how often the behavior occurs. Unfortunately, self-monitoring is also challenging for people with ADD because of their difficulties with attention and distractibility. However, that doesn't mean you can't do it. We suggest the following exercise to get you started on self-monitoring by becoming more aware of what you are doing.

1. Pick a day or two for self-monitoring.
2. List one or two of the problem behaviors on which you want to focus.

Table 2.3 Self-Check: Environments That Help and Hinder Attention

Conditions	+/−	Environments	Examples
Sounds		Quiet	
		Soft music	
		People talking	
		TV on	
		Machinery	
		Traffic	
		Heating system	
		Other	
Sights		Blank walls	
		Windows	
		Pictures on walls	
		Clocks	
		Low lighting	
		Fluorescent lights	
		Other	
Smells		Food	
		Cleaning supplies	
		Paint	

Perfume

Cigarette smoke

Automobile fumes

Other

Time of Day

Early morning

Afternoon

Early evening

Late at night

Location

Outdoors

Small room

Large room

Library

Basement

Office

Home

Other

Interactions with Others

Frequent socializing

Frequent telephone calls

Limited socializing

Limited telephone calls

None

3. During that one- or two-day period, write down when, where, with whom, and in connection with what activity the problem behavior occurs.

For example, you may discover that many of the problems you have because of your ADD become worse at the end of a tiring day or in a noisy, chaotic environment. You may find that you don't work well on a team but that you excel when you're on your own. You may find that you work more easily on some tasks than on others. Monitoring problem behaviors to find out specifically when and where they occur can help you prevent them.

Use Your Strengths to Bypass Weaknesses

Earlier, we asked you to identify your strengths. Now you need to start using these strengths to help you solve problems. Here are some examples of ways to use your strengths to help you with your weaknesses:

- Tap your creativity to develop new strategies or several possible solutions to a problem.
- Put your visual strengths to use by drawing pictures and diagrams, or build mock-ups to help you solve problems.
- Figure out a way to use your enthusiasm to help you complete boring tasks.
- Take advantage of your verbal strengths to talk yourself through a problem.
- Visualize the end product to help you develop a plan of action. (We discuss how to implement this invaluable tool in Chapter 3.)
- Access your social/professional network for any resources or referrals you need.
- Ask a good friend to encourage you to finish a necessary but boring task.

Using Self-Awareness to Prevent Problems

Becoming self-aware is another key strategy and the first step in self-improvement. If you are not aware of a problem, you cannot fix it. On the other hand, if you are aware, for example, that you have difficulty working under certain conditions, you will be able to avoid those conditions. Likewise, if you are aware that certain people rub you the wrong way, you can plan to avoid those people. Avoiding these situations translates into problem prevention.

We hope these checklists have made you more conscious of your strengths as well as your weaknesses. Many of the problems you experience as a person with ADD are dealt with in this book. If you are aware of a problem, simply look it up in the table of contents and turn to the appropriate section, where you'll find several strategies you can use to help prevent the problem from occurring. However, be sure to read the next chapter first. It will provide you with the tools to get you on your way to managing attention and getting organized.

3

Your Personal Toolbox

EVERY GOOD WORKER needs tools to help him or her do a good job. Whether you are a mechanic, an engineer, an artist, a homemaker, or a computer consultant, you need to assemble a toolbox containing every-thing you'll need—screwdrivers, wrenches, brushes, flashlights, and so on—to enable you to do your job effectively and efficiently.

This is particularly necessary if you have ADD. Not only do you have to assemble the tools of your trade, but also you have to develop or invent other (personal) tools to assist you specifically with your ADD. Just as people with poor eyesight wear glasses to help them read, people with ADD need strategies to help them overcome their everyday problems. The research-based tools that are introduced in this chapter will help you do just that.

Visualizing, self-talk, routines, checklists, and the Stop! technique are the primary tools you will use throughout this book as you begin to bring your attention under control and organize your life. The problem-solving strategies in the remaining chapters all utilize these tools.

Important Rules for Using the Tools

As any good mechanic, artist, cook, or computer technician will tell you, it is important to know what your tools can do and how to use them before actually starting a job. Following are some guidelines to keep in mind as you learn how to use these tools:

- Proceed slowly. Start small. Remember, "Rome wasn't built in a day."
- Familiarize yourself with one tool at a time.
- Try using the easiest tools first. For many people, this means starting with learning to use checklists (Tool 5), because checklists are familiar to most of us.
- Try out your new tools in several different situations.
- Combine tools for greater effect. Once you have familiarized yourself with each of the tools separately, you can start combining them for a more effective outcome. For example, you can use self-talk (Tool 1) to remind yourself to use a routine (Tool 4) for a specific task.
- Practice using these tools several times daily, at first.
- Learn only one or two routines (Tool 4) at a time and turn them into habits before trying to learn another new routine. Start with simple routines.
- Personalize checklists (Tool 5) and routines (Tool 4). You can add or subtract items on the list, according to your needs, or invent new checklists and routines based on particular needs. For example, if you're driving in a car pool, you can develop a pickup routine based on where each person lives in relationship to where you are coming from and where you are going.

Tool 1: Self-Talk

Self-talk is exactly what it sounds like: talking to yourself. You hear young children doing it all the time (e.g., "Mustn't touch," "No, no," "Good girl"). Remember the children's book *The Little Engine That Could*? This story offers an excellent example of self-talk. "I think I can. I think I can. I think I can," said the little engine encouragingly, as he chugged slowly up a steep hill. And, "I thought I could. I thought I could," said the little engine with pride, as he succeeded in conquering the slope.

As children grow older, self-talk becomes internalized. As adults, many of us talk to ourselves a lot of the time, but we are often unaware that we are doing so. We refer to the process as "thinking things through" or "weighing the options." We give ourselves "a pat on the back."

Unfortunately, we often use negative self-talk, too. How many times have you said to yourself, "I know I'm going to screw this up"? Self-talk can act like a self-fulfilling prophecy: if you tell yourself you are going to screw up, you will. On the bright side, you'll also find that positive self-talk works the same way. If you tell yourself you are going to do your best, you will.

Keeping the Message Positive

More specifically, positive self-talk includes the following applications:

- Asking yourself questions and answering yourself in order to think things through (basically, arguing with yourself)
- Describing something verbally to yourself in order to help you remember it
- Self-instruction (telling yourself what to do, how to do it, and when)
- Self-encouragement (e.g., "I can handle this," "I won't give up," "I'm almost done") in order to maintain your motivation to start and finish a task
- Self-monitoring (asking yourself, "Do I understand this?" "Am I making progress?" "Am I paying attention?") before instructing yourself to either continue doing something or change what you are doing
- Remembering lists of things (to buy or to do) and where you put something

Listen to yourself and become aware of the self-talk you are already using. Are you using negative self-talk? If so, try to change the message to a more positive statement. In Table 3.1, we provide examples of self-talk that you can use when encountering some of the problems that come with living with ADD. Once you become more conscious of what you say to yourself in the form of questions and answers, you can expand on these comments and use self-talk in more and more situations.

How to Use Self-Talk as a Memory Aid

If you do not already talk to yourself, it is best to begin by talking out loud to yourself, in your own room or another private space. Then, as you become more proficient, you will be able to internalize your speech (or at least mutter under your breath). In order to remember a piece of information using self-talk, you will have to repeat whatever it is you want to remember several times. The first exercise in this section helps you practice self-talk, and the last two exercises will help you increase your memory skills by adding self-talk to visualizing (Tool 2).

When shopping or running errands:
1. Before leaving your house, repeat aloud three to five items you want to buy at the store. Repeat them again on the way to the store.
2. See if you can remember them when you get to the store.
3. Try this with more items. Practice this same technique by repeating aloud three to five errands you want to complete in the next few hours.

After being introduced or meeting someone for the first time:
1. Repeat one time out loud the name of someone to whom you have just been introduced. (You can say, "Hi, Jane Doe!")
2. When you move on, repeat the name twice to yourself.
3. Visualize the person as you repeat the name.

Table 3.1 Examples of Self-Talk

Behavior	Self-Talk
Focusing Attention	"Stop! Pay attention."
	"Am I paying attention?"
	"Move to a quieter place. It's too noisy in here."
	"Did I hear the directions? I'd better ask and pay attention this time."
	"Am I too tired to focus? I'd better take a break."
Managing Anger	"Stop. Think."
	"Stop! Take a deep breath before saying anything."
	"I don't have to get angry when she says that."
	"I'm getting tense. Relax."
	"What is happening here? Why am I angry?"
	"I can deal with this later."
Managing Impulsivity	"Stop. Think."
	"Stop! Make a plan."
	"Slow down."
	"Stop! Look at all the choices before deciding."
	"Read the directions slowly and carefully."

continued

Table 3.1 *(continued)*

Behavior	Self-Talk
Increasing Motivation	"Boy, will I feel great when I finish this!"
	"This is hard, but I think I can do it."
	"This will take only fifteen minutes if I really concentrate."
	"When I'm finished we can go to the movies."
Coping with Failure	"I can handle this."
	"Failing doesn't mean I'm stupid."
	"What can I learn from this?"
	"I'll try again tomorrow."
	"I won't give up. I'm going to keep trying."
	"Maybe I need some help with this one."
Solving Problems	"How should I go about doing this?"
	"What, exactly, is the problem?"
	"I'd better write all the things I will need to do in order to solve the problem."
	"I can solve this if I go slowly and systematically."
	"What are all the possible solutions?"
	"What would happen if I tried this?"
	"Should I try a different strategy?"
	"What is getting in the way of solving the problem?"

When going to a new place:
1. Repeat aloud three to five times the route from your house to a new place.
2. Visualize the route you are going to take.

Tool 2: Visualizing

Visualizing is a way of thinking. We tend to believe that we can think only in words, but in actuality, many people use visual images in their thought processes. Visualizing can help us accomplish the following objectives:

- Improve our memory
- Relax
- Keep the end goal in mind
- Become inspired and motivated
- Solve problems
- Rehearse and prepare for a potentially problematic situation
- Find our way to (and back from) a new location
- Find objects that we have misplaced

Many of us are unaware that we already think in pictures. Inventors and physicists often create images in their minds of the structures they want to build. So do architects and artists, and so can you. Learning a sport can be greatly enhanced through visualizing. Football coaches and golf instructors often tell their students to visualize themselves performing certain moves in order to play better.

Our friend Betty learned how to ski by using visualizing techniques. Her instructor suggested the following five-step process:

1. When you are on the slope, find a person who skis the way you would like to ski.
2. Watch that person ski.
3. Close your eyes and visualize that person skiing.

4. Then ski down the slope visualizing yourself skiing the way the person was skiing.
5. Follow this person down the slope. Visualize yourself making the same moves.

Visualizing can take place in your head—or on paper. Have you ever traced a route on a map or circled something important on a list? Maps and lists are visual ways of conveying information. Drawing a star next to an important detail in an article and using an arrow to relate one piece of information to another are also visual ways of conveying information. Throughout this book, we will help you to use visualizing to predict a potential problem, organize information, make decisions, help you remember, and set goals.

Meanwhile, it is necessary to hone your visualizing skills. Practice with the following exercises and become an observer as well as a visualizer. Notice the color, size, mood, and movement of particular objects, scenes, or people.

When we tell you to close your eyes and visualize a particular image, you may say, "But when I close my eyes, I don't see anything." You don't actually have to see a picture per se. Perhaps we should use the word *imagine* instead of *see*. In these exercises, try substituting the word *imagine* for *visualize*, if you are having difficulty.

Using Familiar Images to Begin Visualizing

It is helpful to begin visualizing with images you have already seen. Visualize a room in your home, a friend's face, or yourself at work. When you do this, ask yourself some questions:

- Can you see the furniture in the room? the window? the door?
- Can you see the color of your friend's hair and eyes? What is your friend doing?
- What are you working on? Are you feeling successful or frustrated?

These are the kinds of visualizations you can practice standing in line at a bank, for example.

Focusing on Details

We talk more about finding things in Chapter 4. Right now, though, you can use the following exercise to start practicing incorporating visualizing for problem solving.

1. Pick up a book or cup.
2. Look at it carefully. (Notice details such as color, shape, and weight.)
3. Put it on the table and walk away.
4. Close your eyes. Can you see yourself putting the book or cup on the table?

When you visualize yourself walking to your car or preparing breakfast, be sure to focus on details. You can also practice by creating detailed visual images of any of the following subjects:

- The sequence of steps you take to make yourself breakfast
- Your keys (e.g., how many, shape, use)
- A speaker at a conference you attended, looking calm and competent
- The route you take to work or to a friend's house

Tool 3: Hearing, Touching, Smelling, Tasting

Hearing, touching, smelling, and tasting are other ways of knowing that can add power to our thought processes. Using these other senses can also help us increase our memory and solve problems. For example, feeling the shape of the pill on your tongue or using your sense of taste can help you remember if you have already taken your medication.

Spend some time developing each of these senses. For instance, you can spend a day focusing on your sense of smell. Smell everything: your toothpaste, your shampoo, clean clothes just out of the dryer, your kitchen, your office, your car, and so on.

Tool 4: Routines

You can practice using tools such as self-talk and visualizing in your daily life before using them to solve problems. Routines, however, are more difficult to master and must be learned only one or two at a time.

A routine is a related series of steps that you follow regularly in order to complete a particular task. Routines can become habits and, as such, require little thinking or expenditure of emotional energy on your part. When a routine has become a habit, you don't have to ask yourself, "What should I do next?" Your body already knows what to do. Routines free up your mind so that you can focus on something else. Most of us have already developed our own routines (habits), such as how and when we take our medication, the route we take to work every day, or the way we iron a shirt.

Learning a new routine can take time, but once you've learned it, you no longer have to think about it. If you have driven a car with a stick shift for a while, you know that you do not have to consciously think about how to do it: your hands and feet automatically do the right thing out of habit. This was not at all the case when you first had to learn how to shift gears. That took some time, a lot of thought, and a lot of practice. The same is true of riding a ten-speed bicycle. Beginners have to painstakingly learn how and when to change the gears and activate the brake, but frequent bike riders hardly ever pay attention to those things. Routines can become so habitual that we often find ourselves thinking (or daydreaming) about other things as we do them. Have you ever driven to work and wondered how you got there? Driving to work by the same route each day can become such a habit that we no longer consciously think about it as we go along.

As you think about some of your habits or routines, you may discover that some of them are efficient and effective, while others are inefficient and ineffective. The routes we habitually take to work or for shopping are not necessarily the shortest and most time-saving. Our habitual way of cleaning the house is not necessarily the most efficient.

While you should keep the good habits you have created, the routines presented in this book can become replacements for some of your bad ones. For example, if you are like other people with ADD, you may spend an inordinate amount of time trying to get through your day. Many of the things you are required to do in the course of the day can be turned into habits that will save you time and energy. Here are a few examples of tasks and actions that can be turned into routines:

- Locating your keys when you want them or parking your car where you can find it (Chapter 4)
- Organizing your kitchen (Chapter 5)
- Getting to appointments on time (Chapter 6)
- Paying your bills or getting ready for a trip (Chapter 7)
- Taking your medication as prescribed (Chapter 9)

Remember that you can learn only one or two new routines at a time. Each new routine requires several weeks (or longer) of practice before it becomes a habit and you no longer have to think about it. Many routines are included in this book under specific problem areas that people with ADD experience.

Tool 5: Checklists

When beginning a new routine, it is helpful to write out the list of tasks involved in the routine in order to remember them. Almost all of us write lists for ourselves at one time or another, but actually using these lists is another story. Generally, we know that making a list before we go shopping can help us remember what to buy, but checklists can serve many other purposes. They can be used to itemize steps in a routine, as just noted, as well as parts or components, travel directions, recipes, or any other items you want to remember for whatever purpose.

Checklists can also comprise steps or actions that must be followed in sequence in order to complete a larger task. In these types of checklists, each small task can be checked off when it's completed. Here are some relevant examples of checklists:

- Daily "to do" lists (Chapter 6)
- Requirements of a grant proposal for work (Chapter 6)
- Items to pack for a trip (Chapter 7)
- Time lines for completing a project (Chapter 7)
- Menus and shopping for a dinner party (Chapter 7)

Checklists can help us conquer deadlines and measure our progress toward a goal. Above all, checklists can decrease our stress and uncertainty and greatly increase our efficiency. This book is filled with lists and checklists to help you both at home and at work, and you can begin using many of them to solve problems almost immediately.

Tool 6: Stop!

The final tool discussed in this chapter is the Stop! technique. Often the life of a person with ADD is filled with frustration, irritation, fear, and worry. These feelings can get in the way of solving problems no matter which major tool or set of tools the person is trying to use. Being able to stop these feelings or hold them at bay will allow you to achieve success in solving your problems using the tools in our kit.

Saying the word *stop* focuses your attention and drags it away from distracting thoughts and feelings, including daydreaming. Many times, if something goes wrong, people with ADD press the panic button, even if the problem is relatively minor. Pressing the panic button and falling apart does not help you solve problems or overcome barriers. In fact, it wastes a lot of time (and leaves you exhausted). You can use the Stop! technique when you find yourself spinning your wheels and getting nowhere. Tell yourself to "Stop!" loudly and firmly.

We tell ourselves to stop when negative thoughts and feelings threaten to overwhelm us. Saying the word *stop* is like tuning out the static on your favorite radio station so that you can listen to the message loud and clear. It is similar to turning off the electricity before beginning to repair an appliance.

When using the Stop! technique to stop negative thoughts and feelings from interfering with what you are doing, it is often helpful to add some of the examples of self-talk from Table 3.1.

Stop! Technique: To Calm Down

Often, in addition to saying "Stop," we tell ourselves to calm down, slow down, or relax. Calming is difficult to learn and requires much practice. However, calming has a reciprocal relationship with the other tools. When you have achieved a certain amount of mastery using the other tools, you will become calmer and have less stress. The calmer you are, the easier it is to use the other tools. Calming is a combination of self-talk, visualizing, and various relaxation techniques. Calming techniques include the following:

- Telling yourself to stop and take a deep breath before trying to solve a problem
- Taking a break from stress by visualizing yourself in a relaxing situation (e.g., on the beach or in a hammock)
- Visualizing yourself acting in a calm and deliberate manner
- Doing physical exercises, especially before or as a break from a difficult task or situation
- Motivating yourself through self-encouragement and rewards
- Counting to ten before responding
- Meditating before tackling a problem

When using self-talk to calm yourself down, think of yourself as talking to your best friend. Think of what you would say to your friend if she was frustrated and this feeling was interfering with her work. Perhaps you would tell her, "You're right; that was really annoying. But you can't let it get in the way of your work." Sometimes you might have to be firm with your friend to break the hold these emotions have at the moment.

If you are frequently anxious, angry, or depressed, you should consider consulting a psychotherapist. A therapist can help you understand the reasons for your negative feelings.

Stop! Technique: To Remind Yourself to Follow a Routine

Before routines become automatic, it is all too easy to forget to use them and to fall back into bad habits. Try these exercises to help you get into the habit of using Stop! to focus your attention when you're developing a new routine:

- When making a withdrawal from a bank or an ATM, as soon as you get the money, immediately tell yourself, "Stop! Count the money."
- When you are finished brushing your teeth, immediately tell yourself, "Stop! Screw the cap back on the toothpaste tube."

Stop! Technique: To Stay Focused

Saying "Stop" is a particularly important tool for people with ADD who are constantly trying to do two things at once or who flit from task to task. It is also a tool that you can begin using immediately—and using often—whenever you have difficulty screening out distractions. For example, if you catch yourself daydreaming or notice your attention wandering, tell yourself to "Stop!"

In this chapter, we have introduced the six most important tools you can use as you strive to overcome some of the problems associated with

ADD. Other tools that can help you solve specific problems are introduced in the appropriate chapters. Using the six major tools can make big changes in your life by helping you approach problem solving in a more effective and efficient manner. It is our hope that you will feel a sense of control you may never have experienced before.

PART II

Practical Strategies for Everyday Problems

4

Help, I Can't Find My Keys!

ALMOST EVERY MORNING, *as his wife watched in alarm, Dan would spend a frantic forty-five minutes trying to find his keys, his wallet, and the papers he had brought home from work the previous day. "Can you believe it?" he would say. "I can't find my keys. How can you just sit there? Why don't you help me?" he would shout. But as his wife had learned, Dan's keys could be anywhere. They had been found on a shelf in the bookcase, in the refrigerator, on the bathroom floor, on the night table in their daughter's room, and on the picnic table, to name only a few spots. Neither Dan nor his wife had a clue as to where they might be. He couldn't remember when he'd had them last or what he'd done with them. And he couldn't get to work without them.*

This story with slight variations is repeated daily in thousands of households across the country. One of the biggest problems a person with ADD has is losing things. Losing your keys, glasses, or wallet can be annoying and frustrating—if it happens only once in a while. Losing things almost all the time adds a tremendous amount of stress to your life. Even if you changed little else, finding your keys, wallet, and glasses when you need them would improve your life dramatically. You would save a lot of time—and eliminate a lot of stress.

Why You Keep Losing Things

Research tells us that in order to remember something later, it is important to focus our attention on it so we can get it into our "working memory." With ADD, you can have great difficulty focusing your attention. You are often distracted by noises (loud and soft), movement, and the many activities going on in your environment. You can even be distracted by your own thoughts!

The minds of people with ADD are often filled with many wonderful and not-so-wonderful deliberations: solving problems at work, inventing a new way to do something, worrying about an upcoming dinner party. If you cannot keep these and other distractions under control a large part of the time, they will interfere with your ability to focus your attention on such concerns as where you are parking your car or putting your keys.

Often people with ADD lose their belongings because they are trying to do two things at once, and this kind of multitasking usually means not doing either one well. You cannot focus long enough on either task to get both into your working memory. If you are thinking of something else while you are putting your keys away, you will not remember where you've put them. It's as simple as that.

Preventing Items from Getting Lost

The trick to finding needed items is to prevent them from getting lost in the first place. No, we're not going to tell you that you must put each little thing in its place all the time! That sounds oppressive (even though it works). We *are* going to tell you that the reason you lose various items is that you are not focusing your attention on them when you have them in your hand and you are not focusing your attention on what you are doing with them.

How to Stop Losing Your Keys

There are three practical strategies you can use to prevent you from losing your keys:

- Attach them to your body in some way so that you always have them with you. We suggest that you buy a retractable key chain, lanyard, or bungee. Attach your keys to your purse or belt with a chain, and voilà! Your keys will always come trailing after you if you try to leave them someplace.
- Learn how to focus your attention on your keys when you have them in your hand. Routine 1 will help you execute this strategy effectively.
- Always keep your keys in the same place — not everyone's favorite strategy, but it does work if you designate a place near the door to put or hang your keys when you get home. Routine 2 is designed to get you in this habit.

Routine 1: Focus Your Attention

This first routine helps you focus your attention on your keys and where you are putting them so that you will be able to locate them quickly and easily. You will be using self-talk and visualization, and you should practice this routine slowly and deliberately.

1. Every time you pick up your keys, feel them carefully and tell yourself, "I can feel my keys in my hand."
2. Look at the keys again, blocking out any other thought, and tell yourself to pay attention.

3. Tell yourself, "I am putting my keys in my purse" or "I am putting my keys in the box on the table."
4. Visualize yourself putting the keys in the specified place as you are doing it.
5. Keep practicing this routine daily, each time you use your keys, for two weeks or until it becomes automatic.

Routine 2: Put Them in the Same Place

This next routine uses tips to help you get into the habit of putting your keys in the same place every time.

- Always keep your keys in the same place when you are not using them. Do not put your keys anyplace else, even for a second.
- Select a place that is in plain sight (not behind or under something) and that is close to the door you must unlock when you enter the house. This could be a box placed on a table near the entrance or a hook on or near the door. You may have to select one place at home and one place at work.
- Always return your keys to the same place immediately after unlocking the door or turning off the ignition of your car. Don't allow anything to interrupt the routine—even if you are carrying heavy packages and want to put them down, the phone rings, or you have to run to the bathroom!
- Practice returning your keys to the same place immediately after using them for at least two weeks until it becomes automatic.

In this way, your keys will be either in your hand; in a lock, such as on the door of your house, the ignition of your car, or your office door; or in the place you have chosen to put them when you are not using them.

Important tip: Never carry around just one key. You are more likely to lose one key than a bunch of keys on a ring. Add something bright to the key chain to help you locate the keys more easily in the dark depths of your purse or backpack or if you accidentally throw them on your desk.

How to Stop Losing Your Glasses, Wallet, or Cell Phone

Routines similar to the preceding one can be used for your glasses, wallet, or cell phone. When you are not using these items, they should be placed either in your purse (or backpack or briefcase), in a pocket of something you have on, or in a carefully selected place in your home or office.

It will be easier if you keep your keys, wallet, and cell phone (as applicable) together in the same place. All three of them could be hung from hooks by the door or placed in a box on a nearby table. You could also buy yourself one of the new electronic locators that function much as a car door opener or TV remote. You press a button on your locator, and the disk attached to your keys will beep until you find it.

Glasses can be worn around your neck or placed in a spot that is related to where you use them. For example, if you read in bed at night, you could put your glasses on the nightstand; if you wear your glasses when you work at the computer, place them on the desktop. Glasses may be moved from desk to nightstand as needed, but you should limit the number of places they can be to two or three. If you must take them off when you answer the phone or when your eyes are tired, be sure to place them in your designated spot or on your desk or nightstand.

Some people with ADD who use reading glasses get several pairs. They are then able to place one pair on the nightstand and one on the desk (and maybe another pair in the car) so they don't need to move the glasses from place to place. If you can't see without your glasses, be careful when you take them off: stop and note where you are putting them. If you don't note where you are putting them, you won't be able to find them—because you can't see them with your glasses off!

Important tip: Be sure to *feel* the item carefully when you have it in your hand, and *tell yourself* that you are holding it. This will help you become more aware of the item in your hand. *Tell yourself* where you are putting it, and then *visualize* where you are putting it. This will help you remember where you placed the item.

How to Remember Where You Parked Your Car

Milly emerged from the mall laden with packages. She was triumphant. She had finally finished buying all her holiday presents! Now all she wanted to do was go home and collapse with a nice cup of hot chocolate. But her triumph turned to tears as she spent the next forty-five minutes, still lugging her packages, trudging back and forth in the snow looking for her car. There were many things she could have done with those wasted forty-five minutes that would have left her in a much better frame of mind!

Does this story sound familiar? Finding your car in a large parking lot can be almost impossible if you don't remember where you parked it. The following routines can help you remember where you parked your car. Once again, prevention is the key.

Routine 1: Locate Your Car in Parking Lots You Frequently Use

In parking lots or parking structures that you frequently use, park your car in the same place every time. This means that you have to choose a space that is usually vacant when you arrive. Such spaces are bound to be relatively far away from where you want to go; they're the ones people usually pass by on their way to parking as close as possible to their destination. However, if you park regularly in one of these spaces, not only will you be able to locate your car, but also the walk will do you good! You can do the same thing when you park in the structure or lot near where you work.

Now when she drives to her local shopping mall, Milly always parks between Sears and Marshall Field's in parking place 61 near the south entrance to the mall, regardless of where she plans to shop. The only time she finds another car in that particular spot is the day before Christmas—and on that day, there are usually no open parking places anywhere else in the mall either.

Routine 2: Locate Your Car in an Unfamiliar Parking Lot

1. When you have to park in a lot you haven't used before, park near a landmark (a tree, a lamppost, the very end or beginning of an aisle, etc.).
2. When you get out of the car, *stop*, look around you at the landmarks, and *tell yourself* where you have parked the car.
3. *Visualize* your parking place.
4. Just as you are about to enter the mall or elevator, *stop*, turn toward the parking lot, and spot your car.
5. *Tell yourself* which direction you will have to turn when you exit the mall or elevator to get to your car.

Routine 3: When Parking at the Airport

1. Whenever you park at the airport, *stop* as soon as you get out of the car and look around you.
2. Locate floor number, parking section, space number, and landmarks.
3. *Tell yourself* where you are parked, before you walk away.
4. Write your location on something you will be keeping with you, such as an e-ticket receipt, a planner, or note paper.
5. Just before you enter the elevator, stop, turn around, and spot your car. *Tell yourself* the direction you must turn from the elevator when you return from your trip, and write this down.
6. Note which elevator you are using, and be sure to use it when you return.

How to Stop Misplacing Your Money

Every time Dwight checked his wallet, he seemed to have less money than he thought he had. He never could imagine where his money had gone. He tried remembering what he had bought during that day or week, but it never added up. He often thought that his money had been stolen somehow or that a clerk had given him the incorrect change.

Dwight's problem was that he rarely put his money in his wallet. When he bought something at a store, he just shoved the change into one of his pockets. He did the same thing wherever he went. Eventually, of course, the pockets overflowed, especially since they had toothpicks, stray pieces of paper, napkins, and other stuff crammed in as well. At home, this was a bonanza for his wife. Whenever she was short of cash, she just walked around the house scooping up dollar bills wherever Dwight had dropped them. People on the street or on the bus were equally as happy.

Vonnie, too, lost money, especially when she went shopping. As she neared the cash register, she would take out a $20 bill to pay for her purchases. But on the way, she would see something else she wanted and would run over to get it. By the time she finally got to the cash register, the $20 was gone. Unfortunately, this was not a onetime occurrence. Vonnie has also lost her credit card on more than one occasion.

If you are like Dwight, you must learn to put your money in your wallet all the time, and if you are like Vonnie, you must learn not to pull your money out until the very second you have to hand it over to the checkout person. Keep reminding yourself to do this several times during each shopping trip. Notice that both Dwight and Vonnie fail to pay attention to the money they have in their hands. If you are having similar problems with holding on to your money or credit cards, go back and practice Routines 1 and 2 in the "How to Stop Losing Your Keys" section in this chapter.

How to Stop Getting Lost

Alice not only gets lost when she has to drive somewhere but also has gotten lost inside her son's school. Once when she was shopping in a department store, she got so turned around that she had to ask her three-year-old daughter to help her find the way out. She jokes that when she was in college attending football games, one of her friends had to go with her to the bathroom in order to help her find her way back to her seat in the stadium. Since Alice's new consulting job requires her to travel a lot, this is becoming quite a serious problem for her.

Getting lost all the time is a symptom of Alice's ADD. She does not pay attention to her surroundings. Are you one of those people who are always getting lost like Alice? Once again, this is due to problems with focusing attention on what is important and screening out distractions. If you are like Alice, there are four related strategies you can use to prevent yourself from getting lost:

- Buy a compass for your car at an auto supply store.
- Get area maps of the routes you have to travel.
- When you are driving to a new place, get in the habit of focusing your attention on the landmarks and signs around you in order to orient yourself.
- *Repeat aloud* the names of the landmarks and signs you are passing (e.g., "Waterloo gas station on the left"; "High school on the right").

Routine 1: Getting to Your Destination

After installing the compass in your car, start practicing this first routine.

1. When confirming your next trip, ask your contact person at the other end for directions to the site and important landmarks to look for.
2. At least a week before you leave on your next trip, get a map of the area, and circle where you will be leaving from and then your destination.
3. Looking at the beginning and ending points, highlight the route between the two points, taking into account the directions you got from your contact.

4. Note the direction in which you will be traveling throughout (north, northwest, east, first east and then north, etc.).
5. As you drive, check your compass frequently (and compare it with your map) to make sure you are going in the right direction.

If you are fortunate enough to have a global positioning system in your car, it can trace routes for you. Similarly, you can get maps of your route from the Internet. In any case, you still need a large paper map of the area that includes both the starting and ending points of the trip in order to understand the direction in which you will be traveling. This map should have enough detail for you to find an alternate route to your destination if you encounter construction or a major accident along the road.

Routine 2: Driving Home Without Getting Lost

Getting lost when returning from your job can sound unbelievable to many people. "Just retrace your steps," they say. But if you have ADD, you know that retracing your steps is easier said than done. To avoid getting lost when coming home, follow the tips in this routine and keep a pad or notebook handy.

1. As soon as you park at your destination, get out of the car, *stop*, and look around.
2. *Tell yourself* where the car is parked.
3. Look at the way you came into the parking lot and *visualize* the way you should turn out of the parking lot or structure to start home, and *write it down*.
4. *Visualize* the turn you made at the intersection preceding your turn into the lot.
5. *Tell yourself* which direction to turn at this intersection when you are going home, and write it down.

Generally speaking, at this point the rest should fall into place. Again, as you drive home, check the compass frequently to make sure you are going in the right direction.

The instructions you give yourself during self-talk help focus you on the landmarks and signs. In this way, you can find your way back by looking for and recognizing the landmarks.

Routine 3: Finding Your Way on Foot

Similarly, self-talk can also help you find your way out of department stores or other large buildings.

1. As soon as you enter the store, *stop* and look around.
2. *Tell yourself* about the visual cues around you. For example: "I'm entering the store at children's shoes"; "I'm passing women's lingerie." These directions will help you find your way out of the store when you want to leave.
3. If you can't remember all the markers you passed, ask someone to direct you to the store entrance near children's shoes, women's lingerie, or another specific site.

When Something Is Already Lost: Finding Misplaced Items

Since we're only human, we will lose things occasionally. (People with ADD, though, can be more human than others in this way.) If you do lose something, despite all your good intentions and efforts, there are several strategies you can employ to help find the lost item:

- *Visualize* what the item looks like: size, color.
- *Visualize* yourself with the item.
- Try to remember when and where you had the item last.
- If you can't remember, use logic. *Ask yourself,* "Why would I have had the item in my hand? Why would I have used this item? What could I have been doing with it?"
- If you are still having difficulty locating the item, slowly start to *visualize* your day from before you had the item until now.

■ Progress Report: The Importance of Slowly Building Your Skills

Milly benefited greatly from using only two routines mentioned in this chapter. In addition to parking her car in the same spot whenever she goes to the mall, she started attaching her keys to her purse with a bright orange bungee (you have to have a sense of humor to do that!). Milly says, "It's a miracle! Being able to find my keys and my car has added almost an entire hour to my day!"

Dwight and Dan are trying to change too much too soon. Dan is trying to put his keys, wallet, and cell phone in the same place every day—with modest success. Although some people could do all three at once, Dan needs to work with one item at a time and practice the routine for two to three weeks before trying the same routine with a second item. Dwight, too, is struggling to focus his attention, constantly trying to do two things at once. Both Dwight and Dan insist that they can do this, but those who live with them know better.

Alice was amazed to find out how well talking to herself worked. She was also surprised at how little time each routine took her and how easily the routines became habits. An added benefit is that she has become much more aware of her surroundings—she really *sees* things now.

- Don't panic; take a deep breath and calm down.
- If you start to get frantic, tell yourself to *stop* and think this through.
- *Ask yourself*, "Could someone else have used it? Could someone else have moved it?"
- Stop thinking about it, or "sleep on it." Get involved in something else. You may remember after you have rested your mind a bit.

Guidelines to Help You Locate Things Without Panicking

- Accept the fact that losing some things will always be part of your life.
- Assume that you will sometimes forget where you have put something.
- Assume that, most of the time, you can use your brain to help you figure out where you have put something.
- Recognize the importance of focusing your attention.
- Recognize the importance of practice, practice, practice.
- Realize that prevention is the key to not losing items in the first place.
- Become adept at self-talk and visualizing.
- Remember not to panic.
- Learn only one strategy or routine at a time.
- Realize that if you use the tools presented in this chapter, you will not only find the item you need but also save yourself a lot of time—and grief.

5

My House Is a Pigsty!

HAVE YOU EVER WALKED into a house that was spotless? Everything is put away neatly. No newspapers and books are lying around. In fact, there are no bookcases. (These people probably don't read much.) Have you looked into the refrigerator and found—almost nothing? (These people tend to eat all their meals out.) The living room looks so well ordered—until you realize there is very little furniture. There are no pictures on the wall, no plants. They have no children, so there are no toys scattered about. Yes, the house is neat—but would you want to live there?

If you describe your own living space as a pigsty, you need to ask yourself if it truly is that bad or if you just have unrealistic expectations of what a home should look like. Most of us have an idealized image of how a house, room, or office should look. We see pictures in magazines that look so beautiful—and neat. If only we could have a house like that! What we don't consider is that those pictures have been staged, those people have lots of money and can employ several maids, and those houses are so large that each dish or cup can have its own drawer!

Barriers to Neatness and Organization

There are many causes of clutter and mess in a house—the first of which is the act of living in it. A certain amount of clutter or mess is inevitable—if you are alive. Another reason our houses and offices become easily cluttered, whether or not we have ADD, is the lack of adequate storage space to put everything away in its own special place. In addition, most of us have neither enough time to keep a house neat day in and day out nor enough money to hire someone to keep house for us or a personal secretary who can straighten our office. Finally, we are a generation that accumulates "stuff," as we are easily tantalized by the profusion of products advertised almost everywhere.

ADD, by its very nature, imposes barriers to neatness and organization. Here are some examples of behaviors that contribute to the pigsty look:

- Always rushing and not taking a few seconds to put things back in their place
- Impulsively sticking things anywhere without thought or planning
- Poor skills in classifying or categorizing, resulting in failure to group items that are similar or related
- Constantly overcommitting oneself, leaving no time to plan or organize
- Distractibility—thinking of three things at once and thereby short-circuiting the intention to follow through with a task, or losing interest in an object after using it and forgetting about it or not noticing where it gets stashed
- Procrastination—delaying putting something back or straightening something out until later

Is All Clutter Bad?

If your home works for you (and your family), it is, by definition, not cluttered and disorganized, no matter what it looks like. Of course, what works for you may not work for someone else. One of the problems in addressing this subject is that people tend to be judgmental and to compare themselves (and others) against some old-fashioned ideals.

Don't worry about what other people think. Don't worry that your house doesn't look like something out of *House Beautiful* or *Woman's Day*. Don't worry that your house is not as neat as your mother's or your friend's. Your house should be convenient for living and working, easy to maintain, and a reflection of your interests and personality.

Can Some of Us Work Well Amid Clutter?

Clutter doesn't have to be a problem as long as it doesn't get in the way of your being productive. Those of us who work largely with ideas can function perfectly well amid a certain amount of physical clutter. Some of us who are visually oriented can remember where we have put every last piece of paper and thus never lose anything—even in a cluttered environment. Those of us who have good internal organization can continue working even if the external environment is cluttered.

When Is Clutter a Problem?

> Peg didn't pile her personal papers all over the house. She stashed them in old grocery bags. She even separated the bags, somewhat. She kept one of them upstairs in her bedroom, and she kept the documents she needed for her tax return in a bag under her desk in her home office, next to her wastebasket. She told herself a few times that stowing important documents in a brown paper bag wasn't a good idea, but she never found the time to do anything about it.
>
> A few days before April 15, Peg finally decided it was time to do her tax return. She reached down under her desk to

retrieve the bag stuffed with her financial records and . . . it wasn't there! After an hour or so of hysteria, Peg accepted the unavoidable truth: the bag was not in the house. It had been thrown out. She dimly recalled that she and her husband had gone on a cleaning spree a few weeks before, and she had forgotten to warn her husband about the bags.

If there is no place to sit down and no space at the table to eat, if dirty clothes are draped over the living room sofa and green things are growing in your refrigerator, if you've lost all the papers you need to file your income tax return and you trip over someone's shoes on your way to the bathroom—then clutter is a problem for you! Unfortunately, it took losing all of her tax documents for Peg to realize that she had a serious problem when it comes to getting organized.

If you think you may have the same issues that Peg had, the following list of indicators can help you determine if you could use some organizational strategies. Clutter is a problem for you if:

- It interferes with health or safety.
- It affects task completion.
- It affects speed or accuracy.
- It interferes with your ability to protect yourself from legal or economic harm.
- It leads to constant bickering with others.
- It makes you depressed or anxious.
- There are piles of papers on every horizontal surface.
- You try (and fail) to cram three sizes of clothing into your closet (in case you lose or gain weight).
- Stockpiles of frayed towels, single socks, old jars without lids, broken things, and other items of questionable use are scattered around your house.

Is There One Way to Organize Things, to De-Clutter?

The best style of organizing—among the many options available—depends on your personality, values, and lifestyle, as well as on the size and use of the space in question. A small space might need more rigorous organization than a large space so that everything will fit; in this case, installing lots of shelves may be a practical remedy. If you have young children in your house, it will be harder to keep it neat and tidy. In this case, it would be wiser to ease up a little on your requirements for neatness than to run yourself ragged trying to maintain the same standards you had before your children became part of the household.

Anything goes, if it fits your needs, when it comes to your private spaces at home or at work (such as your desk, study, closet, office, or workstation). On the other hand, public spaces (or areas accessible to or used by others, either at home or at work) require shared decisions on the part of all the users. Examples are entrances, hallways, the family room, conference rooms, lounges, and shared rooms such as offices, bedrooms, kitchens, and bathrooms. It is inconsiderate and disrespectful to clutter or mess up a shared space. This is where clutter can get you into trouble if the others who share the space do not have the same standards as you do.

Action Steps to Get Organized

The larger goal should be to have a room, house, or office that's relatively neat and convenient to use, and one that reflects the personality and interests of its owner. The goal should not require you to spend such a large amount of time on cleanup that you have no time for your responsibilities to your family or for yourself.

Visualize and Plan

First, you need to *visualize* what you want the space to look like. Ask yourself, "Is this realistic? Is this me?" Modify your visual image, if necessary. Be sure to give yourself time to think and plan before beginning any task. Here's how to approach the job:

- Set a large goal and break it up into small intermediary steps. You can use visualization to help you with this.
- Decide how you will keep yourself motivated and focused.

- Decide on and locate any materials or tools you will need to work on the task.
- Think the task through from beginning to end. Decide on strategies you will use.

Make a Schedule

It will be helpful for you to make a schedule. Set aside regular time each week to work, such as forty-five minutes to an hour twice a week. Then record these sessions on your calendar and daily "to do" list. (We cover this in Chapter 6.) Work for the agreed-upon time each session, and then stop and go on to something else. That way, you'll be fresh the next time you plan to work on de-cluttering.

Maintain Motivation

Maintaining motivation as you work on your de-cluttering can be difficult. Many of us enthusiastically start an improvement plan and then slowly let it fall by the wayside. Strategies to get and keep you motivated include the following:

- Break up your goal into small steps. Make each step a mini goal—something that will take you forty-five minutes to an hour to complete. You'll be surprised how quickly the time will go and how much you can accomplish in such a short period.
- Write a daily contract for yourself and use it as motivation. Specify the goal for the day, how much time you will work, and how you will reward yourself. Sign it.
- Plan to have a friend help you or just keep you company.
- Reward yourself for your effort and the progress you make toward your goal. Plan a major reward for reaching your goal.

Decide What to Throw Away

Every organizing/de-cluttering task involves both throwing things out and rearranging the things you need to keep. This means you need to prepare yourself to make decisions—some of them rather painful. For example, you may have to throw out your old computer that has been sitting unplugged on the floor of your study, covered in dust. Or, you may have to throw out the beautiful, old, broken-beyond-repair radio that you saved from your first apartment. Prepare yourself for those decisions now so that when the time comes, you can make them on the spot. Tell yourself to get rid of the following:

- Things that are broken beyond repair
- Things you haven't used in the past two years
- Magazines more than six months old
- Newspapers more than one week old
- Clothing you haven't worn in more than one year
- Toys your children haven't played with in the past year
- Things of which you have duplicates
- Old boxes, jars, unmatched socks, and single mittens
- Old things you have replaced with newer versions
- Gifts that you have never used—or liked
- Catalogs more than a month old

Plan to throw out these things before you actually get to them—because the minute you see them, you will want to keep them. Keep telling yourself: "I must throw these things out. I do not have room for them. I will not be able to reach my goal if I keep them." Visualize your goal to keep you motivated.

Steps to De-Cluttering and Organizing Your Room

The first step in the de-cluttering process is to look at your room and take a visual inventory. What types of "stuff" do you have in the room (e.g., books, papers, clothes)? Decide where you want to put these items. Do you have enough space to put things away? Do you have enough shelves for your books, enough hangers for your clothes, enough storage boxes for other things that you do not use often but feel you need to keep?

Make a Plan

Before you start organizing, equip yourself with all the things you think you'll need to get rid of the clutter. These may include bookcases, large plastic garbage bags, storage boxes, filing cabinets, file folders, paper clips, and even a shredder. In addition, locate a charity such as the Salvation Army or the Purple Heart to which you can donate usable items that you no longer need—and think about how happy you will make someone.

Then you have to decide on your strategy. Either start with putting away all the items in one category (e.g., books), or start with one corner of the room and put away everything in that corner. With this latter strategy, you can divide your room into a grid with tape or colorful yarn and then clear one section at a time.

Separate Clutter into Simple Categories

In the beginning, you can make just a gross separation of the materials. For example, put all books in one pile, all papers in another pile, and clothes in another. (Keep in mind that the strategy you use to get your room under control is not the same strategy you will use to maintain your room.) You should throw some things out as you sort, but the main goal at this stage is to separate your "stuff" by category.

Next, turn your attention to one pile of "stuff"—for example, clothing—and separate this large pile into three smaller piles:

- Garbage
- Items you use frequently and plan to keep
- Things to give away or donate

You can also designate an additional pile of items that you cannot decide whether to throw out or keep. Make this pile as small as possible.

Attack Each Category One at a Time

Throw out the things that must be thrown out. Use your garbage bags for this. Put in storage anything that you need to keep but will not be using often; these can go in the garage, basement, storage closet, or similar location.

Put the items you use frequently where they will be accessible to you—such as in your bedroom closet, in a dresser drawer, on a kitchen shelf, or in your desk. Tie the garbage bags and dispose of them, and hang up or put away the clothes you plan to keep (or arrange the books you plan to keep on shelves). If you have a pile of things you plan to give away, immediately put them in a box or clearly labeled garbage bag and move it to the front door.

If you have an undecided pile, you can let it sit where it is for the time being—if you have the available space—and tackle it in a day or two when you are feeling strong and ruthless. Always keep reminding yourself about and visualizing the larger goal. Keep telling yourself that you must throw things out to make room for the things you really need. Then divide the undecided pile into (1) garbage, (2) give away, and (3) storage.

Finally, pat yourself on the back when you have reached your goal for the day (even if the room still looks somewhat messy). If you've used tape to section off the room, you should be able to see bare floor in the section you've just finished! Seeing a bare floor can be a big reward in itself.

Attacking a Pile of Papers

Many people with ADD have piles of paper on every horizontal surface of the house: the kitchen table, the piano, the top of the TV, guest beds, the floor—everywhere. These piles can contain bills, uncashed checks, old financial statements, catalogs, advertisements, insurance documents, birthday cards, letters, invitations, recipes, photographs, and more, all jumbled together.

You work with a pile of paper the same way you work with the other things in your room. First, you separate it into three smaller piles:

- Garbage—including all junk mail, advertisements, catalogs you don't use, old birthday cards, and the like.
- Current—including bills, checks, invitations, and tickets. This is the pile you need to act on in the near future.
- Safekeeping (storage)—including tax documents, financial statements, check stubs, house and car insurance, user's guides for appliances, paid bills, and so forth. This safekeeping "pile" contains important items that are up to date and need no further action from you.

You might have a fourth pile of business-related documents.

In an ideal situation, you will end up with a really large pile of garbage. If you can't decide whether to throw something out or save it, put it aside until a time when you are feeling ruthless.

Think "Inside" the Box

Before beginning work, buy or collect some boxes, baskets, or other suitable containers in which to keep all of your sorted-out piles of papers. You'll likely need three small containers for (1) your current papers, (2) undecided and unsorted papers, and (3) safekeeping of important documents. Label this last storage box with the current year; at the end of the year, tape the box shut and start a new storage box for the new year.

You can fine-tune this process somewhat by putting your recipes in a recipe drawer in the kitchen, pinning invitations and tickets to a bulletin board, and putting all your photographs together in a drawer in your bedroom. You can also start filing your important papers in your file cabinet as follows:

- Manuals and warranties for appliances and electronic equipment
- Contracts

- Financial statements
- Insurance documents
- Paid bills (gas, electric, water, etc.)
- Tax documents

Routine for Opening Your Mail

When you open your mail each day, be sure to have a wastebasket or garbage bag at your side. Make it a daily routine to immediately toss catalogs you don't use, advertisements, and other junk mail in the trash.

Organizing Your Kitchen

Kitchens tend to get cluttered easily because they are the most used room in the house—by everyone. A lot of this de facto clutter can be prevented through organization. There are many ways to go about it, depending on your needs, your lifestyle, the size of the space, and the size of your family, among other factors. Whatever your circumstances, organization of one type or another is important if you want to save time and energy—in this, the work center of your home. Start using the strategies in this section to get your kitchen in order.

First, make sure that the things you use most often (cooking utensils, everyday dishes, glasses, pots and pans, etc.) are the easiest to get to. This means that your good dishes, company silverware, pottery mugs, and linen tablecloths can even be stored or displayed outside the kitchen, if need be.

Second, make sure that the things that go together are near each other, if possible. For example, dishes, cups, and glasses should be in the same or adjacent cabinets. Likewise, all foodstuffs should be in the same or adjacent cabinets. Keep a garbage pail near the garbage disposal under or near the sink.

Third, keep in mind that there are two centers of activity in the typical kitchen: one that incorporates the sink/dishwasher and one that incorporates the stove. Things you use for cooking should be near the stove (including food, utensils, pots and pans, and plastic wraps). Things that get washed should be near the sink/dishwasher (including dishes, glasses, and silverware), as should the garbage pail and dishwasher soap.

There are several ways to organize your spice shelves to save yourself time. For example, Marvel, who is petite, keeps the spices and seasonings that she uses regularly—such as salt, pepper, and cinnamon—in the front of the shelf. John puts his spices in alphabetical order. Chrissy divides her spices into sweet (the ones she uses to make cakes and other desserts) and savory (the ones she uses to jazz up meat and vegetables). By organizing their spices, these three friends of ours avoid having to spend fifteen minutes rooting through a jumble of bottles and tins every time they want to locate a particular ingredient.

Routine 1: Keeping the Kitchen Neat and Organized

Once you've organized your kitchen, you've lightened the chore of keeping it clean and uncluttered. To maintain a clutter-free kitchen, you can initiate some new routines.

1. Label the cabinet shelves with what they hold (e.g., cereal, pasta/pasta sauce, vegetables, soup, coffee/tea/filters).
2. Every day, make a conscious effort to put things back on the right shelf when you are finished using them.

Routine 2: Making Cleanup Easier

Every day as you cook, be sure to put every item away as soon as you are done using it. For example, when you are finished putting some pasta in the pot to boil, immediately reseal the package and return it to its designated storage place. When you have finished adding a can of tomatoes to the sauce, and while you still have the empty can in your hand, immediately place the can in the garbage. When you are finished using a mixing bowl (and while you still have the bowl in your hand), immediately put it in the sink to be washed or in the dishwasher. Consider this routine as part of the cooking process.

Routine 3: Finding Your Focus in the Kitchen

To focus your attention on what you are doing, refer to the routines for putting away your keys and wallet in Chapter 4. Whenever you pick up something in the kitchen, do the following:

1. Tell yourself you have it in your hand.
2. Feel it in your hand.
3. Use it for whatever purpose you intended.
4. If you are going to use it again, place it on the counter in front of you.
5. When you are finished using it and while it is still in your hand, tell yourself to put it where it belongs.

Tips for Maintaining a (Relatively) Neat Home

You may already have a relatively organized home but still find it hard to keep it neat and clean. Here are some ideas to put you on the right track.

Set Some Realistic Standards of Cleanliness and Neatness

Health and safety standards should be a priority; other standards may be nice but not necessary. Discuss standards for rooms used by everybody (family/roommates) as opposed to one's private room. For example, the members of the household might agree that individuals should not leave their clothes lying around the living room at any time but may leave clothes lying around their own room, as long as they put them away at night.

Share Household Chores

Everyone has different standards and priorities, as well as busy schedules. Try to be flexible and not let housecleaning get in the way of loving family relationships. Negotiate household chores based on each person's strengths and interests. Remember, people with ADD have difficulty performing daily, repetitive tasks, as well as completing tasks once they have begun. They are best at tasks that require problem solving and those that require a certain amount of creativity and excitement—such as figuring out how to wash the outside of the third-floor windows. Others in the family may not mind the boring tasks as much, because it gives them time to think or to relax. In addition, children often like to run the vacuum cleaner. They think of it as a toy. Other children enjoy the responsibility of taking the garbage out.

It is important that each person choose the chore(s) for which he or she will be responsible. Chores should be described specifically. The general phrase "Clean the living room" could give rise to arguments if one person's idea of cleaning the living room is merely picking up the newspapers while another person believes that vacuuming the rug and dusting the tables and lamps are part of the job. A time frame for each chore should be agreed upon and noted on a calendar. Checklists of chore specifics can be posted on a bulletin board, and the chores can be exchanged each week at a family meeting.

Additional Ideas for Maintaining Cleanliness

In addition to setting realistic goals, compromising, and sharing chores, the following are some simple rules for maintaining a (relatively) organized home:

- Hire someone to help clean the house every week or two, if you can afford it. Sometimes this is the best money you can spend.
- Set aside—on the calendar—a once-a-month cleanup/fix-up day for the family. Turn it into a pizza party.
- Locate a coach from your local ADD organization to help you with disorganization and clutter. (In the "Resources" section at the back of the book, we list some organizations that can help you find support groups and coaches.)
- Shop for supplies at stores that have large inventories of boxes, shelving, file cabinets, and other accessories to help you organize

your home. Examples are Target, The Container Store, California Closets, Home Depot, and Lowe's.

Despite your best intentions, ADD makes you particularly vulnerable to clutter and disorganization. You will always have to exercise vigilance and control over your tendency to drop things wherever you are instead of placing them where they belong.

At the same time, we want you to stop being ashamed of not having a picture-perfect home. In a warm, comfortable home, a certain amount of clutter is inevitable and acceptable. Set realistic goals. Get help with organizing, if you need it. Adopting our simple routines and telling yourself to focus on putting something where it belongs will go a long way toward preventing clutter.

6

No Matter How Hard I Try, I'm Always Late

FRANK DESCRIBES HIMSELF *as a last-minute kind of person. In fact, he secretly enjoys "cutting things close." If he has to meet a deadline, he almost always comes through, even if he has to stay up all night. "I run on adrenaline," he says. However, when it comes to arriving on time for his son's football game, responding to phone messages promptly, or returning a borrowed book after reading it, don't count on Frank. His coworkers aren't crazy about his "just in time" behavior either. It makes them nervous. They have complained to their boss about Frank's not being a team player.*

Bunny, on the other hand, is late for everything, regardless of deadlines. She gets up an hour earlier than she has to in order to get ready for work. It takes her some time to decide what to wear, and she often has to go searching for a report that she needs to take back to the office. It even takes her a while to decide what to eat for breakfast because she stops to watch a news item on television. (She turns on the television each morning to keep her company.) Then, she suddenly looks at the clock and realizes she is going to be late again!

Both Bunny and Frank have ADD, and both are in danger of losing their jobs because of it. If you have the same problems as these two, you know that chronic lateness is high on every employer's list of "no-no's." You are also aware that if your time-management problems affect others at your workplace, your employer has an added impetus to fire you. In this chapter, we delve into how ADD affects your ability to manage time at work and at home, and we suggest exercises, routines, and strategies to manage your attention, increase your time-estimation skills, efficiently plan your schedule, and overcome some common time wasters so that you can get to places on time!

Poor Time Management Can Cause Multiple Problems

In addition to negatively affecting your work, time-management problems can have a profound negative impact on your personal relationships. (This subject is discussed more fully in Chapter 8.) It is true that you may be able to arrange some accommodations at work for your chronic lateness. Bunny, for instance, takes assignments home with her at night to make up for the times she is late, although her employer is not really happy about this. Also, departmental meetings can sometimes be scheduled to start a little later in the day in deference to a valued employee who is known to be chronically late. However, regardless of accommodations, time-management problems at work can be irritating and stressful for others.

People who can't successfully manage their time often fall behind in their work and often must leave important things undone, due to the inevitable time crunch. Time-management problems caused by ADD take many forms. For example:

- Frequently missed deadlines, appointments, and meetings
- Chronic lateness for work and appointments
- Difficulty wrapping up final details of projects
- Procrastination; difficulty getting started on tasks
- Overcommitment due to impulsively saying yes to all requests
- Difficulty estimating how much time a job will take

The fallout from these problems can cause you considerable anxiety and stress. You often feel that there is something looming over your head that you need to do. You rarely experience the relief of "catching up," and you often feel driven and out of control. At home, problems with time management lead you to feel as if you're constantly letting your family down.

Manage Attention to Manage Time

For people with ADD, the major hindrance to their ability to start and finish things on time is their difficulty in focusing on the task at hand. If you are not focused on what you are doing, it can take you three times as long to start and complete it, robbing you of precious hours and opportunity. Therefore, you need to make it a priority to manage your attention and screen out distractions, as much as possible. Give these proven strategies a try:

- Tell yourself, "Stop! Pay attention." Or ask yourself, "Am I paying attention?"
- For a complex task, make a list of the steps required and check each one off as you complete it.
- Use a daily "to do" list to help you plan your day. Check off tasks as you complete them.
- Work on difficult or complex tasks when you are most alert. This could be early in the morning, midday, or maybe after a workout.

- Develop some strategies to keep you from losing important items so you won't have to spend time searching for them. (Go back and review Chapter 4 if you need to.)
- Take frequent breaks. Come back and refocus.
- Be sure you're working in a nondistracting environment.
- If you must work in a noisy area, try listening to soft music to help screen out the noise.

An Exercise to Improve Self-Awareness

You also must develop an awareness of how often your attention wanders while you work. In order to do this, you can practice the following exercise for about an hour or so, two or three times a week, for several weeks:

1. Decide on a relatively boring activity or task to work on.
2. Set a timer to go off in five or ten minutes, and then begin working on your chosen assignment.
3. When the alarm sounds, ask yourself if you were on task at that moment.
4. Return to the work at hand and tell yourself to refocus.
5. Repeat steps 2 through 4.

Becoming aware of how often your attention wanders will give you a real advantage in learning to manage your attention.

Self-Talk to Focus and Maintain Attention

Here are some suggestions of what you could say to yourself under various circumstances once you have identified when your attention has wandered:

- "Stop thinking about your upcoming travel plans. Start working on that project."
- "Don't stop in the kitchen to straighten up. You need to get out of the house on time."

- "Don't stop to pick up the cleaning now; you'll be late for the kids."
- "If I'm on time, then the meeting can start on time, and everyone will go home on time."

Increase Time-Estimation Skills to Manage Time

Generally, people with ADD have a poor sense of time. When they are busy or involved in something, they have little comprehension of the passage of time. They are often late to appointments because they underestimate how long it takes them to prepare before leaving as well as how long it takes them to get there.

Poor time estimation detracts from the quality of your home life as well as your work life. For example, Gabe, a dad with ADD, is often late for supper, much to his family's annoyance. Sandy, a stay-at-home mother with ADD, rarely has meals ready for her children. It's not uncommon to hear them wail, "Mom, I'm hungry."

An Exercise to Improve Time Estimation

Good time estimation is a core skill. It helps you get to work on time. It helps you prioritize and schedule tasks and helps you plan your day and use your time efficiently. Therefore, it is important to do all you can to develop that skill. The following routine will help you hone your time-estimation skills:

1. Every day or several times a week, estimate the amount of time you think a particular task or activity will take. (You can do this as a sort of game: estimate how much time it takes you to select your clothes and get dressed to go out, prepare and eat breakfast, get to work, etc.).
2. Time yourself as you complete the task or activity.
3. Check to see how accurate you were and what interfered with your accuracy.

4. Try it again.
5. Check to see if you were more accurate this time.
6. Try it again.
7. Ask yourself, "What can I do to estimate time more accurately?"

How to Get to Appointments on Time

Getting to work or appointments on time depends on making relatively accurate time estimations. First, you want to estimate how long it usually takes you to get dressed to go out. Is it five minutes, fifteen minutes, half an hour, or more? Make sure you include brushing your teeth, taking a shower, drying your hair, deciding what to wear, applying makeup, gathering anything you need to take with you, and other preparations. Then estimate how long it will take you to get to the appointment from your home.

Next, make a list of the following questions, and answer each one as accurately as possible.

1. What time do you have to be there?
2. How much time will it take you to get there?
3. What time do you have to leave your home in order to get there on time?
4. What time do you need to start getting ready in order to leave on time?

When you leave your home, do not stop on the way for any errands. Unplanned-for errands make you late. They always take up more time than you had imagined.

If you are going to a new place, give yourself an extra ten minutes or so to get lost and find your way again. If you think you might have trouble parking, give yourself an extra five to ten minutes. If you anticipate a lot of traffic, give yourself an extra ten or fifteen minutes. Include these conditions in your list as part of the time it will take you to get where you are going.

Self-Talk for Better Time Management

The best time-estimation skills can go out the window if you allow yourself to get sidetracked on your way to an appointment. In order to profit from your time-estimation skills and get someplace on time, keep reminding yourself:

- "I look unprofessional when I am late."
- "I make mistakes and have accidents when I am late."
- "I am insensitive and rude to others when I am late."
- "No errands along the way."
- "I will just go out the door. I won't answer the phone."

A Routine to Help You Leave on Time in the Morning

If you tend to dawdle in the morning before you leave for work, you can move many of the activities you must do before you leave to the night before. The following routine, done the night before, will help you improve your time estimation and get out of the door on time in the morning:

1. Decide on *all* the clothes you will wear, including underwear, socks, shoes, jewelry, coat, and so forth, and set them aside. (You can help your children select their outfits the night before as well.)
2. Prepare your lunch (and your children's lunch), if necessary, and store it in the refrigerator.
3. Place anything that you need to take with you near the door.
4. Be sure your keys are near the door (or in your purse or briefcase).

Do this every night before you go to sleep until it becomes your regular habit. You'll notice a remarkable change in your attitude when you feel that you are not rushing every morning to get out the door.

The Importance of Planning for Better Time Management

When Patti went back to school to earn her master's degree in the evenings, she decided to take two courses each semester in order to finish as soon as possible. But at the end of the first semester and before she had started her term paper, her three-year-old got pneumonia. Then, in the middle of the second semester, she twisted her ankle and missed a week of classes. When the third semester rolled around, a major new project came in at work, and she had to put in overtime to finish it. As a result, Patti learned that although it had seemed as if she could manage two courses a semester, in reality, she could complete only one.

Planning, an integral part of time management, would have helped Patti tremendously. You can plan your activities for the day or week, your steps for completing a project, your route when you go shopping, and many other procedures. Although you may say that planning itself takes up time, the amount of time you save by planning before doing something can be enormous. Planning helps you achieve the following objectives:

- Minimize or eliminate zigzagging around town in search of items you want to buy.
- Complete work projects on schedule by reducing the amount of time you spend going back over details you have omitted or done incorrectly.
- Ensure that you have the materials and resources you need to start and complete a project—or bake a cake!

Unfortunately, planning, which is an executive function, is not a strength of most people with ADD because they are often too distracted to plan. They have trouble focusing long enough to plan effectively, so they just give it a lick and a promise. Often impulsivity interferes with planning, as people with ADD just forge ahead without thinking. Sometimes people with ADD assume they are too busy to plan. Yet, planning can save time and make the difference between the success and failure of any task.

Before tackling any job, large or small, always tell yourself, "Stop! Make a plan." Then, in order to develop the plan, ask yourself such questions as these:

- What am I trying to do?
- What is my goal?
- What will it look like when I'm finished?

Get an Overview of What to Do

When planning, first, you try to see the big picture. Then you break the whole down into the steps you will need to achieve the goal. Visualize yourself as you go about the tasks needed to complete the project. At work, you can use the planning sheet in Figure 6.1 as a guide.

When planning, always build in some thinking time. Allow five minutes each morning, noon, and night to review and revise your plans. In addition, you'll want to build in some personal crisis time. A crisis can easily throw off any well-planned schedule—and crises, like Patti's, do occur.

Create "To Do" Lists

"To do" lists, planners, and calendars can be your best friends. You can't function really well without them. They can help you pay your bills by the due date, ensure that you renew any licenses before they expire, keep your appointments, and get more done in less time—while giving you the luxury to have some fun and relax.

Therefore, first you need to take a few minutes at the beginning of each day (over morning coffee, for example) to write your daily "to do" list. (You could also write the list the night before.) In a brainstorm mode,

Figure 6.1 Work Project Planning Sheet

Today's date: _____

Finish/due date: _____

Number of days to due date: _____

Number of hours I will put in per day: _____

What is this project about? (describe it) _____

_____

_____

_____

Who is going to review this project? What do they want me to do?

_____

_____

_____

What will the finished project look like?

_____

_____

_____

How will I go about doing this? (general plan of action)

_____

_____

_____

Materials needed:	Where found:	When to get:
_____	_____	_____
_____	_____	_____
_____	_____	_____

Help needed—what/who:

_____

_____

_____

Steps from start to finish:

_____

_____

_____

■ Sample "To Do" List

One of our clients made the following "to do" list and prioritized the tasks to make sure she did the most important ones first.

(2) Call Lamont

(1) Go to bank

(1) Gym 6 p.m.

(3) Work on speech

(2) Call Marvin

(1) Buy dog food

(1) E-mail Joe

(1) Arrange flight and hotel

---

write down everything you need to do or want to do that day. Then prioritize the list, assigning numbers one through three, as shown in the sidebar sample.

1 = This must be done today.
2 = I'd like to do this today if I have time.
3 = I can easily do this some other time.

Review the items that must be done today—all your number-one items—and schedule times during the day to do them, using your new time-estimation skills. Then fill in the unscheduled time with the items you would like to do—your number-two items. And so on. Leave some time for last-minute must-do items. As the day progresses, you may think of some more items to plug in. Check or cross out items as you complete them.

A Routine for Writing Daily "To Do" Lists. Remember that routines are among the most effective time-saving strategies you can master. As we discussed in Chapter 3, using routines can save time by eliminating the need to make decisions and figure out what to do next. Try any of these next three options to help you get in the habit of creating daily "to do" lists:

- Write your daily list as you drink your first cup of coffee in the morning.
- Write the list first thing on arriving at work—right after hanging up your coat.
- Write the list the night before, as you get ready for bed.

It can be helpful to review and analyze your list at the end of the day to see how realistic it was.

Remind Yourself About Must-Dos. Although the things you must do each day already appear as priorities on your "to do" list, you can never have too many reminders of the essentials on a given day. For example:

- Picking up your son's birthday cake for his party this afternoon
- Gassing up your car before going to the airport to pick up your friend
- Mailing your grant proposal so that it will beat the deadline

It can help to post reminders of must-dos in logical places throughout your house—on the front of your coat (so that you will see it when you put on your coat to go leave), on the front door (so that you will see it before you walk out), or on your steering wheel (so that you will see it when you get into the car).

Make a Calendar

Making a monthly calendar can be incredibly helpful for organizing your life. You should do this on the first day of the month (or the night before). Be sure to write down all appointments, activities, vacations, deadlines, and so forth, and schedule one day each month for paying bills, renewing licenses, and doing car and home maintenance. Figure 6.2 shows a sample calendar from one of our students.

Figure 6.2 Sample Calendar

January

Sunday	Monday	Tuesday	Wednesday	Thursday	Friday	Saturday
1		**2** 11 am: Appt with psychologist Laundry	**3** Go shopping Go to cleaners, bank, post office, gas	**4** 9 am: Yoga Laundry	**5** 9 to 12:30: Work on projects 2 pm: Pick up Jan	**6** Clean house 1 to 3 pm
7 3 to 5 pm: Correspondence/filing/clean desk	**8** Go shopping Go to cleaners, bank, post office & gas	**9** Laundry	**10**	**11** 9 am: Yoga Laundry	**12** 9 to 12:30: Work on projects 2 pm: Pick up Jan	**13** Clean house 1 to 3 pm
14 3 to 5 pm: Auto maintenance & repairs	**15** Go shopping Go to cleaners, bank, post office & gas	**16** Laundry	**17**	**18** 9 am: Yoga Laundry	**19** 9 to 12:30: Work on projects 2 pm: Pick up Jan	**20** Clean house 1 to 3 pm
21 3 to 5 pm: Household repairs and maintenance	**22** Go shopping Go to cleaners, bank, post office & gas	**23** Laundry	**24** 1:30 pm: Appt with DDS	**25** 9 am: Yoga Laundry	**26** 9 to 12:30: Work on projects 2 pm: Pick up Jan	**27** Clean house 1 to 3 pm
28 3 to 5 pm: Write out checks for rent, utilities, telephone, credit cards	**29** Go shopping Go to cleaners, bank, post office & gas	**30** Monthly expense report due 6 to 7 pm: Family haircuts	**31** School conference			

Using a weekly planner can give you a good overview of your week and allow you to schedule special jobs and activities based on the amount of time you actually have available, rather than impulsively saying yes to everything you want to do. With this in mind, every Monday (or Sunday night), make a schedule for the entire upcoming week. Be sure to include taking clothes to the cleaner and picking them up, housecleaning, and food shopping. You can move entries from one day to the next, as needed.

Since the lives of family members are usually interrelated, a family calendar is a must for any parent trying to balance several people's schedules. So, in addition to making a calendar for yourself, you should create a master calendar for the whole family. (You can use the sample in Figure 6.2 as a place to start.) That way, all of you can see where everyone will be and when. For example, if your daughter is depending on you to help her with her science fair project, she needs to know when you will be out of town on business. You can draw up the family calendar at a family meeting once a month.

Completing a Grant Proposal on Time

Many schools and businesses today depend on grants—from the government, foundations, or philanthropic or social service organizations—for a large part of their budgets. Writing grant proposals can be an important part of your job because grants bring in much-needed money for operations, training, and research. However, requests for proposals (RFPs) always come with deadlines for submission, and often there is little time between the day you first hear about the RFP and the submission date.

Writing a grant proposal is almost always something you add on to your regular work. There is typically a mad scramble to beat the deadline, and often that deadline is missed. Therefore, if your job requires you to write grant proposals, or if you think you may be writing a grant proposal, you need to begin work well before you receive the RFP. You may be saying, "How can I begin writing it if I don't know what the proposal is about?" The answer is that all proposals have common elements, and knowing what these elements are allows you to begin addressing them before actually receiving an RFP. Some of us affectionately refer to these elements or sections as "boilerplate." They usually ask you to supply the following information:

- A general description and history of the institution, company, or unit
- Company or institution resources
- Similar projects the company or unit has completed successfully
- Brief biographies of personnel who will be involved in the project

RFPs usually require you to submit the résumés of people who will be working on the project. In order for you to easily fulfill this requirement, all the workers in your unit should update their résumés at least once a year, whether or not a proposal is in the offing. Similarly, letters of recommendation and commendation for your unit, the company, or individuals should be collected throughout the year as projects and activities are completed. These, too, will form part of your proposal package.

In addition, most RFPs require time lines, which help you plan and monitor tasks to be completed. You can develop a generic time line (or chart) that you can adapt for all your proposals, filling in the specific tasks and dates after you get the RFP (see Figure 6.3).

Be sure to have a large wall calendar on hand so that when the RFP arrives, you can schedule all the points of your time line on the actual calendar, making notes of any weekends, holidays, and other days that are unavailable for work.

Dealing with Common Time Wasters

People with ADD face additional barriers to time management in the form of time wasters. Even people without ADD have to be on their guard against the many time wasters at home and at work. You probably recognize some or all of these common time wasters in work environments:

Figure 6.3 Sample Time Line

	Sept	Oct	Nov	Dec	Jan	Feb	Mar	Apr	May	June	July	Aug
Hire staff	X											
Refine plan of operation	X	X										
Develop outcomes of training	X											
Contact advisory board	X	X	X	X			X				X	
Contact trainees		X	X	X	X	X	X	X				
Design instruction/research design		X	X									
Develop assessments		X	X					X	X			
Finalize budget	X	X										
Collect data: pre- and posttests		X	X							X		
Analyze data											X	
Develop graphs and figures											X	
Write and submit report												X

■ How One Woman Handled Her Time Wasters

Bunny made the following list to help her analyze and correct her time wasters so that she could better focus on more important things at home and at work.

Time Waster	Solution
Deciding what to wear to work	Do this the night before so that it doesn't take up time in the morning.
Looking for a report for work	Do this the night before. Put it by the front door as soon as you are done reading it.
Deciding what to eat for breakfast	Eat the same thing every morning or limit your options to two or three.
Stopping to watch TV in the morning	Don't turn on the TV when you are getting ready for work. You might try turning on the radio and listening to some music, instead.

- Telephone interruptions
- Casual socializing
- Long lunches
- Long meetings or frequent meetings
- Unclear priorities/goals
- Unclear responsibilities
- Insufficient information or support
- E-mail/Internet/computer games

At home, in addition to talking on the telephone and impromptu socializing, people waste time running errands and shopping, reading catalogs or magazines, shuttling children back and forth, watching television, and surfing the Net, among other activities.

The good news is that there are simple solutions for many of your individual time wasters. Review the examples just cited of typical time wasters at home and on the job. To increase your awareness of how much time those items (and others) take up in your life, ask yourself questions such as these:

- How long do your phone calls take? (Actually time your next few calls.) How many calls do you make or get (for example, each evening from 6 to 10)?
- How much time does it take you to shop for food each week?
- How often do you run last-minute errands?
- How often do you spin your wheels because you don't have enough supplies, information, or help to do a job?
- How often do coworkers or friends drop into your workspace for an informal chat?

Shopping and Other Errands

Ingrid found that she had to go shopping almost every day because she was always running out of something she needed. Running to a store for even just a few items can actually take you forty-five minutes from the time you leave until the time you return. If you do this daily, it comes to three to five hours of wasted time per week. Try to limit grocery shopping for the family to two hours, once a week, if possible. (An occasional last-minute errand is allowed—if it's really occasional.)

If shopping and running errands take up an inordinate amount of your time, you can greatly shorten the duration by planning thoroughly and making lists. That way, you know exactly what you want to buy and where. Thinking ahead for the week can help prevent you from running out of necessities.

Before going shopping for food at the grocery store, take the time to visualize the meals you are planning to prepare. Ask yourself what items you already have and what items you need to buy for each meal. Be sure to include items such as spices, bread, and butter.

You can also visualize the rooms in your house to help you determine what you need to buy. Visualize your bathroom, and ask yourself, "Do I need . . . " the following:

- Toilet paper
- Hand soap
- Shampoo
- Toothpaste
- Conditioner and other hair products
- Deodorant
- Other

Start your shopping list a week in advance, and add to the list as you become aware that you need something. You can post this list on the refrigerator for easy reference.

Organize your errands by geographic areas, and do the errands that are near each other in succession. For example, if the grocery store, the dry cleaner, and the gas station are within a few blocks of each other, do these errands one after another. Don't go back and forth across town if you can help it. Save the errands in another part of town for another day.

Telephone Calls

If too many telephone calls are a problem, you can let the calls ring through to your answering machine or voice mail when you're busy, and then answer them at your leisure. (We know that not answering a ringing telephone can be a difficult thing to do, but keep reminding yourself that you won't be losing any calls and you will be answering the important ones when you have finished what you are doing.) To help yourself ignore telephone interruptions, you can turn off the sound signal on your phone, knowing that you can socialize on the phone when you have finished what you're doing.

At work, it may be possible to have your telephone calls rerouted to voice mail or to a secretary who can take messages for you.

Perhaps you need to try to shorten your phone calls. If you regularly talk for fifteen minutes or more on the phone, set a timer to help you end your calls in five to ten minutes.

Socializing

Socializing at work can be a terrible time waster. If you work in an office and keep your door open, people will drop in. The solution? Keep your door closed while you are working. This may be hard for you to do since you want to be friendly, but you can leave the door open occasionally or meet your friends in the hallway when you are finished with the task on which you were working. If you work in an open area or cubicle, when necessary you can hang a sign on your workspace such as: "Give me a minute. I really need to finish this." Or you can try what one of our clients did who was afraid of appearing unfriendly. She simply put on a pair of earphones when a job needed her undivided attention. Everyone thought she was listening to something work-related and didn't bother her.

Meetings

Whenever you are in charge of running a meeting, make sure of the following:

- The meeting is really necessary.
- Everyone scheduled to attend really needs to be there.
- It is no more than one hour long.
- The agenda is carefully planned in advance.
- The amount of time allotted to each agenda item is posted on the board.
- The meeting starts exactly on time.

In this way, meetings do not need to take up too much of your time. Putting a time limit on a meeting tends to shorten discussion by encouraging people to stick directly to the point. Allotting a particular amount of time to each agenda item and posting it on the board gives the meeting participants an overview of the meeting and allows them to plan their responses accordingly.

Overcommitment and Overwork

Many of us in this day and age of "go, go, go" are overcommitted. We run from activity to activity, hardly stopping to breathe, and our kids do too. Few of us allow ourselves time to think great thoughts or dream great dreams. Most of the problems stemming from overcommitment that people with ADD experience are caused by their impulsivity. They say yes to everything—impulsively, without thinking, regardless of whatever else they are committed to doing.

Overcommitment leads you to spin your wheels because you don't know where to start or which task should come first. You may flit from one unfinished task to another, trying desperately to finish them all.

Don't Suffer in Silence. If you think you have too much to do at work, whether it is because you have volunteered for too much or because you have been assigned too much, you *must* speak to your supervisor as soon as possible. This may seem somewhat scary, but it will be much scarier if you cannot do what is expected of you and you don't tell your supervisor in time to make the necessary arrangements to get the job done.

If you think you have too much to do at home, you may need to give other people in your family some of the responsibility for the upkeep of the house (as discussed in Chapter 5). Or you may have to rethink what needs to be done, and either eliminate some of your tasks or lower some of your standards.

How to Say No, but Nicely. Some of us are overcommitted because we just want to be nice—to everybody. We have a hard time saying no because we think that if we decline someone's request for help, we will hurt the person's feelings or make the person angry. There are many ways to say no nicely when people ask you to do something. For example:

- "I'm really sorry. I'm just too busy and can't take on any other commitments."
- "I'm tempted to do that, but I don't have time."
- "I'd like to help you out, but I can't right now. I'm working on an important project."
- "I'd like to talk to you, but I'm working right now. I'll call you back as soon as I can take a break."
- "You know I'd rather go to the movies with you, but I promised myself I would start on my project tonight. I'm working on keeping the commitments that I make to myself."

The point is to have the time to do the things you must do. You accomplish this by delegating some tasks to others or cutting down on things that are not of primary importance. Try to eliminate the time wasters that, in reality, contribute little to your overall well-being. And don't agree to help someone unless you have made sure you are not stealing precious time from your family—or yourself.

Perfectionism

Stanley, a manager in a clinical laboratory, was in a part-time MBA program. He knew he could not advance significantly in his career without a graduate degree. Even though Stanley was intelligent and hardworking, writing papers proved a challenge for him. He knew the information and what he wanted to say, but he wanted to do a perfect job. He was afraid to start. He became so anxious that he waited until the last moment and finally had to hand in the paper late. His professor refused to accept it and graded Stanley accordingly. If Stanley had settled for doing an acceptable job rather than a perfect job, he could have handed in his paper on time and received a passing grade. Stanley's perfectionism actually got in the way of his academic success.

Many of us are perfectionists, whether or not we have ADD. Perfectionism can be good if it motivates us to do our best. However, it becomes a burden when we spend so much time polishing a report that we don't have time to finish it, or when we are so worried about doing our best work that we don't even start.

Perfectionism and Procrastination Often Go Hand in Hand

You want something to be perfect and are afraid it won't be, so you don't take the first step. You procrastinate. This cycle of behavior easily becomes self-defeating.

All of us want to do our best. But do we understand that completing a project in the time allotted is as important as doing it well? Many times we need to be content with doing a satisfactory or "good-enough" job rather than a "thrilling" job. We don't need to be perfect or "the best" in everything we do. If you're like Stanley and you find writing difficult, you need to tell yourself that it is OK to write a B paper and then make a plan so that you can hand in the paper on time.

Self-Talk to Overcome Perfectionism. If perfectionism has been a problem for you, you can use the following phrases as self-talk to remind yourself not to let perfectionism get in the way of completing your work:

- "If I don't get this done on time, it won't matter how good it is."
- "I will do the best I can in the time I have."
- "It's OK if this is not my best work, as long as it fulfills the requirements."
- "I won't let perfectionism waste my time."

Plan on Improving Slowly

Time management is extremely important and extremely complex. To make the matter more complicated, each of us has different time-management problems. No one can tackle such problems in one fell swoop. It is best to slowly chip away at the problem. Work on only one aspect at a time. To begin with, you can choose one of the following approaches:

- Make a pledge to be on time for all appointments for one week. Start by being on time for all appointments for the next two days.
- Make a pledge to write daily "to do" lists for one week. Start by writing a list for a day or two.
- Make a pledge to set aside a day each month to pay your bills, and schedule it on your calendar. (We offer a routine for paying your bills on time in Chapter 7.)
- Play games with time estimation for a few weeks. If you have children, try to include the whole family in the game, since time-estimation skills are important for children to learn.
- If you have a family, try scheduling everyone's activities on a large family calendar for one month. This can be a lot of fun and is also a good learning tool for children. You will probably have to correct and update it once a week, which allows for good family time.

7

I Have Things to Do, but I Don't Know Where to Begin

DOLORES WAS IN A PANIC. *Her in-laws were coming the following week. How on earth was she going to manage? She was already putting in long hours on a major project at work. The house was a mess. Why had she let it get so bad? She might have straightened it up last month when she first heard they were coming—and when she had some time—but she didn't. She remembered saying, "I'll do it next week." That was before the new project came in.*

"I'll do it later" is something we all say at one time or other. We often put off boring tasks such as housework, especially if we have a choice of doing something more interesting like going out to dinner with friends. Sometimes we pay quite a price for telling ourselves we'll "do it later."

Many people with ADD habitually put off boring chores such as folding the clothes, washing the dishes, and vacuuming, as they find more fascinating things to do. And the opposite is also true: isn't it amazing how clean your house will get when you have a big project to do for work?

Tasks such as paying bills or giving a speech might make you anxious—and so you put them off. Other tasks, such as repairing a lamp, seem so complicated that you may not even know where to begin—so you put them off, as well.

Procrastination

Procrastination, the habit of putting something off, can be a serious problem for a person with (or without!) ADD. It can result in a house that is chaotic and a lifestyle that is unremittingly stressful. It can interfere with all aspects of your daily life.

Procrastination can delay or prevent you from accomplishing the following things:

- Answering written correspondence, returning phone calls, or responding to e-mail messages
- Paying bills or filing tax forms
- Doing the necessary car maintenance (e.g., gas, oil, repair, license renewal)
- Doing laundry or taking clothes to the cleaner
- Making appointments for medical checkups
- Inviting friends to visit or giving a party
- Packing efficiently and appropriately for a trip
- Doing necessary house maintenance (e.g., having the house painted, having the dishwasher repaired)
- Doing the dishes

By postponing these tasks, you end up with increased costs in penalties or interest for failing to pay your bills when they're due, increased stress because your responsibilities are always looming over your head, missed opportunities when you don't respond soon enough to an invitation or job offer, and worse.

Reasons for Procrastination

Procrastination can be the result of the disorganization and distractibility of ADD. You may allow yourself to get so overcommitted that you do not have time to do everything you need to do, so you keep pushing some tasks to the back of the line. You may dash from task to task as something catches your interest, but the boring chores pile up.

Sometimes you just "can't get around to" doing something that needs to be done because you haven't left yourself enough time or something else took longer than you expected. Or you may have a history of being criticized for every minor error so you are afraid to even start some tasks. Or you are a perfectionist for whom nothing you do is ever good enough, so you don't even try (as discussed in Chapter 6).

A variety of factors can compound procrastination. When the activity is boring, is too difficult for you, has unclear goals or standards, or is either irrelevant, unfamiliar, or highly complex, you may put it off entirely. Your procrastination may also worsen when you are feeling tired, sick, anxious, overwhelmed, stressed, depressed, fearful of failure, or unmotivated, or when the environment at home or at work is distracting, disorganized, disruptive, or lacking in resources or tools.

Anxiety

Procrastination can have a large emotional component. Anything having to do with paying your bills can cause you anxiety if you are chronically short of money or tend to be insecure. While these types of attitudes are best discussed with a therapist, we offer a routine to help you pay your bills on time in the following section.

Overcoming Procrastination

You are most likely to be able to overcome procrastination when the task is interesting to you, you are feeling rested and relaxed, and you have the necessary know-how to do the job. It also is to your advantage to work in a relatively orderly, nondistracting environment and to become proficient in controlling your distractibility for short periods.

Needless to say, few tasks you are required to do daily are very interesting. Yet, it is necessary to do many of these tasks in order to keep your household running smoothly. Planning to reinforce yourself for the progress you make toward completing the task and then to reward yourself for finishing it can motivate you to undertake and complete even the most boring chore. Boring tasks can often be completed relatively quickly in one sitting, if you don't allow yourself to be distracted.

Although you can do many boring tasks when you are tired because they don't require much thought, you should always start a challenging or complex task when you are rested and relaxed. Complex tasks should be done in small chunks. When you feel your mind wandering or when you hit a snag, you should stop and take a break and then come back to the task with your mind refreshed.

If a task seems too difficult, unfamiliar, or unclear, you will need to seek information on how to do it, ask someone for help, or both. Don't put off asking for help because the people to whom you can turn have schedules of their own. You may finally decide that you are not the person to do this task and that you need to hire a well-trained professional. Seeking help is not a failure on your part. It is a wise and responsible decision, if made in a timely fashion.

Getting Started on a Task

Motivation is the key to getting started, as well as the key to being able to control your distractibility. As usual, you begin motivating yourself with self-talk and visualizing, and then plan rewards for accomplishing specific tasks and goals. Use any of the following examples of self-talk:

- "I will feel great even if I just get a good start today."
- "Once I start, I know I'll be able to finish most of it today."
- "It's really easy. I know I can do it."
- "This will take me only twenty minutes if I stay focused."
- "I will really be proud of myself when I'm done with this."

To maintain your motivation, you can visualize yourself working efficiently on the task and visualize the effect when it is completed—such as when the dishes are washed and put away, or when the bills are in their stamped return envelopes and you're carrying them to the mailbox.

Don't forget to plan appropriate rewards for yourself for completing the task. Promise yourself a movie or a dinner out with a friend when the task is done. For a complex task, set simple rewards for each step you complete (e.g., a cup of coffee or a quick call to a friend). When tidying up, you can promise yourself to invite a friend over when you are through. Most important, allow yourself to feel proud when you have completed a task that you have been putting off, and tell your friends about it.

Strategies for Scheduling and Working on a Task

Before beginning to work, you need to break a large task into small steps and make a plan to complete it. It is helpful to schedule steps on your calendar and write daily "to do" lists for yourself (refer back to Chapter 6). You should also decide what materials and tools you will need, and assemble them before you start. Plan to work for a limited amount of time, one to two hours, and be sure to take frequent breaks to recharge your batteries.

Continue using self-talk as you are working, such as: "Just a half hour more, and then I can stop for the day," or "This is taking much less time than I expected," or "I'll take a quick break and then finish it."

Use checklists to help you remember the steps involved in routines or those needed for completing the task, and to see the progress you are making when you check steps off as you complete them.

If you can, team up with others to complete a relatively long and boring task, such as painting a room or filing your papers. Ask a family member or friend to help you or to keep you company as you work. Having someone work with you or just keep you company can make the time go faster and remove most of the stress and anxiety you may have with finishing the task. You can either offer to pay people who are working with you or take them out for lunch after you are finished.

Paying Your Bills

Ingrid once got an emergency phone call from her son just as she was rushing to another meeting. "Mom," the teenager wailed, "there's no water, and I'm in the middle of a shower! Did you forget to pay the water bill again? How could you do this to me?" Ingrid realized that not only had she forgotten to pay the bill but she had ignored the shutoff notice as well. Ingrid often forgets to pay her bills. On top of that, she has run out of necessities such as milk and toilet paper—not once, but often. Admittedly, she is a working mom, but what is she doing with her time that it can interfere so much with her family life?

There are many reasons why people don't pay their bills by the due date—not all of them having to do with ADD. You may think that paying bills is boring, so you put it off. Paying bills may make you anxious, so you put it off. Your life may be so hectic that you can't seem to find the time to pay your bills—or you may be so disorganized that you can't even find the bills themselves. (Refer back to Chapter 5 for how to attack a pile of papers.)

Improving the Setting Can Improve Your Attitude. If tasks such as paying bills are stressful for you or make you anxious, we suggest that you try to make the setting in which you work as restful or inviting as possible. Listening to your favorite tapes or CDs while you pay your bills can help lessen the stress. Paying bills while watching the news on TV can also help take your mind off your anxiety, especially if the program is exciting or engaging. Essentially, what you are telling yourself is, "I hate doing this task, but I am doing it under some of my most favorite conditions." Or you may pretend that you're just listening to the news—and not acknowledge that you are also paying bills. *One caution:* Be careful not to become so distracted by what is on TV that you end up making mistakes in your bill paying!

A Routine for Paying Your Bills on Time. In actuality, it should take only about thirty minutes to pay all your monthly bills, once you sit down to do it. To begin with, as soon as you receive your bills, put them in a special place. Then get into the routine of setting aside one day each month for bill paying. (If most of your bills arrive the first week of the month, a good time to pay bills would be around the fifteeenth.) Then follow these steps:

1. Pick a pleasant, nondistracting place. Turn on some light music.
2. Assemble the bills and envelopes, your checkbook, stamps, and a wastebasket.
3. For each bill you are paying, write out the check, make sure all of the information you entered is correct, and insert the check in the proper envelope, along with the remittance portion of the bill, as appropriate. If you're using a window envelope, verify that the address is displayed correctly.
4. Stamp the envelopes, and immediately post them in a mailbox or place them on a table near the front door for mailing.
5. Save receipts and important inserts and put them in a file drawer. Throw out everything else.

Wherever possible, take advantage of automated bill paying and depositing.

Planning a Trip

It was always amusing to watch Jesse and Sandy pack for their annual trip from Michigan to Aspen. It was so predictable. It took them almost a week. As they tried to cram the Jeep full of the things they thought they would need for their vacation, Jesse would carry something out of the house and stuff it into the car helter-skelter, and Sandy would remove something from the car and carry it back to the house. Then they would reverse roles. By the time they were through packing, they had stopped speaking to each other. They would set off on a lovely spring day, each staring grimly straight ahead. They didn't start speaking again until they reached Kansas.

If you have ADD, the reason you don't start complex tasks can be procrastination, disorganization, or distractibility. You put something off because it is too complicated, you don't know how long it is going to take, you can't focus long enough to sort it out, or it is simply overwhelming. Going on a trip is a complex task. It requires you to look ahead, make many decisions, and manage multiple smaller tasks and details. It can be a source of stress as well as conflict, if it involves other people.

When working on a complex task, the emphasis is on planning — something that is difficult for people with ADD. Careful planning can make the difference between completing the task easily and efficiently — and chaos. Planning for a trip is not just a question of packing your clothes. You also may have to make sure the cat is fed while you're gone, the mail is collected, the heat is turned down, and so on. You need clean clothes to take with you, which means you have to allow enough time to get the clothes cleaned before you pack them. You need to have enough medication with you and enough money to cover the trip. You need tickets if you are going by a public carrier and maps if you are going by car.

Checklists for Planning a Trip

The following checklists can assist you with the planning process. You can personalize the lists to fit your circumstances.

One to two weeks before the trip:
❑ Plan what you will take, using a checklist for each family member.
❑ Check clothing you plan to take: wash, iron, and dry-clean items, as needed.
❑ Arrange for a neighbor or friend to pick up your mail and newspapers, or cancel your newspaper delivery and ask the post office to hold your mail while you're gone.
❑ Arrange for a neighbor or friend to take care of your home and any pets.
❑ Check supplies of medications: make sure you have enough for the trip, and order more if necessary.

Two days before the trip:

❑ Shop for food to take along: bread, fruit, drinks, nuts, cookies, peanut butter, jelly, cold cuts, powdered milk, coffee, trash bags, napkins, paper towels, pet food, and so on.

❑ Select reading material; visit the library for books, tapes, or CDs.

❑ Help children to select toys, books, tapes, and other items to take along.

❑ Pick up clothes from the cleaner and medications you've ordered.

❑ Get any maps you'll need.

❑ Go to the bank and withdraw money for the trip.

One day before the trip:

❑ Pick up additional items as needed.

❑ Pack.

❑ Give your house key to a neighbor or friend who will need access.

❑ Write a note to your neighbor or friend regarding caring for pets, collecting mail and newspapers, watering plants, and other duties, and include a telephone number where you can be reached. Place the note on the kitchen table.

The day of the trip:

❑ Prepare coffee, sandwiches, or other food you want to take with you.

❑ Pack all food, napkins, cups, spoons, knives, trash bags, and paper towels.

❑ Set out pet food, litter, and other pet supplies.

❑ Adjust lights, heat, air, and so on.

❑ Turn off all computers, stoves, coffee pots, and other appliances.

❑ Water plants.

❑ Verify that all doors and windows are locked.

Packing for a Trip

Packing checklists, in particular, must be personalized for your situation. If you'll be packing for a family, each member needs his or her own packing list. Obviously, what you need if you'll be camping is much different from what you need if you'll be touring the big city. Less obvious may be deciding what to pack if you'll be staying with friends versus in a hotel. Do you need to buy yourself a new bathrobe? Many questions need to be answered before you finalize your packing checklist. Will you be packing a lunch, or will you stop for food? Do you need a map of your route? Will you need fancy clothes for a party or the theater? Develop a basic packing checklist that can be used for all trips, or use the following guidelines to create a checklist for a specific occasion:

- Plan how much of each item you will need to take with you. For example, if you will be staying four days in another city, you will need a total of six pairs of underwear (if you don't intend to do laundry)—four for the days you are gone and one for each travel day.
- Plan what you are going to wear each day. Coordinate outfits. Take a blouse or shirt that will match two skirts or suits. Take shoes that will match several outfits.
- When figuring out what to wear for a particular occasion, be sure to include matching accessories. You may need special shoes, stockings, socks, jewelry, belts, hats, jackets, scarves, ties, purses, gloves, or slips.
- Use a partitioned medication box, available at drugstores, for your medication. Count out your medication carefully, based on the number of days you will be gone. Give yourself two to three days' worth of extra pills.
- Make sure to take necessary tickets, work-related materials, and medication with you. If you forget anything else, don't panic. You can always buy items such as combs, toothpaste, and clothing en route or at your destination.
- Attach important items such as medication and tickets to your body in some fashion. This is the best way to ensure that you

won't lose these things. You can use a purse, money belt, pocket, fanny pack, or hanging passport holder.

- Pack the checklist in your suitcase so you can use it again when you are packing to return home. This way, you're less likely to leave any items behind.

The packing checklist in Figure 7.1 is one that we give to many of our clients. It has boxes you can check at the time you are packing each item. There are two boxes, one for the outgoing trip and one for the returning trip.

Planning a Business Trip

The checklist for business trips naturally has more business-related items and is more detailed in some cases. When you develop your own checklists, you can take items from different checklists and combine them to meet your needs.

Important tip: If you wear glasses, always take an extra pair with you on a business trip. One of our clients forgot to do this and was faced with having to give his presentation with one lens of his glasses missing. It had fallen out and been stepped on during the rush of people at the conference registration desk.

One week before the trip:

❏ Plan what you will take, using a checklist.

❏ Withdraw cash: $100 to $200, with $20 in small bills for tips.

❏ Get traveler's checks or foreign currency, if necessary.

❏ Confirm reservations (flight, hotel, car rental, dining, entertainment, etc.).

❏ Locate your business cards and an extra card holder.

❏ Place holds on your mail and newspaper, or ask a neighbor to collect them.

❏ Pay bills that will become due while you are away, to avoid finance charges.

Figure 7.1 Packing Checklist Work Sheet

Leaving on: _____

Returning on: _____

Number of days: _____

Special clothing needed: _____

Traveling clothes: _____

❏ ❏   Tickets

❏ ❏   Medication

❏ ❏   Books/reading material

❏ ❏   Suntan lotion, sunglasses, sun hat, swimwear

❏ ❏   Jewelry

❏ ❏   Belts/ties—list: _____

❏ ❏   Shampoo/setting lotion/hair dryer/brush/shower cap

❏ ❏   Toothbrush/toothpaste

❏ ❏   Razor/shaving cream

❏ ❏   Jackets/coats—list: _____

❏ ❏   Slacks/jeans/shorts—list: _____

❏ ❏   Skirts/dresses—list: _____

❏ ❏   Blouses/T-shirts/sweaters—list: _____

❏ ❏   Underpants/bras/slips/undershirts—number: _____

❏ ❏   Stockings/socks—number: _____

❏ ❏   Shoes/sandals—list: _____

❏ ❏   Nightgown/robe/slippers

❏ ❏   Raincoat/umbrella/boots/hats/gloves

❏ ❏   Laptop, pad of paper, other

❏ ❏   Coffeemaker, coffee, creamer, sweetener

❏ ❏   Camera

❏ ❏   Toys (if traveling with children)—list: _____

❏ ❏   Maps/travel guides

❏ ❏   Food

❏ ❏   Gifts

❑ Select clothing for presentations and try them on. Check accessories.

❑ Purchase extra batteries for electronic devices.

❑ Call your destination and ask to have directions faxed or e-mailed to you.

❑ If you're receiving directions over the phone, listen carefully and repeat each step to confirm that you are correct as you write it down. Ask if there will be construction or other traffic problems in the area. Also be sure to write down the telephone number of the person assisting you.

❑ If you'll be meeting others, exchange cell phone numbers with them so that you can keep in touch as needed.

❑ Arrange for transportation to the airport and home from the airport after your return flight.

❑ Check supplies of medications, and order more if needed.

One day before the trip:

❑ Verify that your driver's license, credit cards, cash, and checkbook are where they belong.

❑ If you're using electronic ticketing, go on the Internet and print your boarding pass. Call the airline to check if your departing flight is on schedule.

❑ Pack plugs and chargers for your laptop, cell phone, pager, cassette recorder, and other equipment.

❑ Pack computer accessories (including memory sticks, disks, keyboard for handheld devices, etc.).

❑ Pack presentation materials, business cards, laptop, slide projector, and anything else you'll need for the session.

❑ Pack any office supplies that may be needed such as paper clips, rubber bands, permanent markers, highlighters, sticky notes, pads of paper, and several large brown envelopes.

❑ Pack clothes.

❑ Count out medication, and put it in your purse or jacket pocket.

❑ If you wear glasses or contacts, take an extra pair.

When you arrive at your destination airport:

❏ Be sure that you have adjusted your watch if you're in a different time zone.

❏ Get a map and study it before leaving the car rental facility.

❏ Ask for directions to your hotel.

❏ Request specific directions for returning the car (time, location, gas tank).

❏ Note how much time it takes you to get from the car rental agency to your hotel.

During the trip:

❏ In your hotel room, keep important things in a special drawer: ticket stub for parking, room key, maps, directions, car keys, wallet, conference proceedings, your presentation materials, and so forth.

❏ Use a large brown envelope to collect all credit card receipts and bills.

❏ Carry an extra card holder to collect new business cards.

Getting ready to leave:

❏ Go on the Internet thirty-six hours before your flight to get your boarding pass for your return flight. Call the airline to make sure the flight is departing on time.

❏ Pack the first thing in the morning, before breakfast (or if it's a really early flight, pack before you go to sleep the night before).

❏ Before checking out, look in all drawers and closets, under all beds, and in the bathroom for any stray belongings.

❏ Put your airline tickets in your purse or jacket pocket.

❏ Check out of the hotel the night before or electronically, using your room TV. Make sure your room key stays active until you leave.

Before returning to the airport:

❏ Allow yourself fifteen to twenty-five minutes to get your car from hotel parking.

- ❏ Add in the amount of time it took you to get to the hotel from the airport.
- ❏ Add in thirty minutes to return the car to the rental agency.
- ❏ Add fifteen minutes to get to the airport entrance from car rental.
- ❏ Total up the amount of time to allow yourself to get to the airport from when you leave your hotel room.

How to Develop Checklists for Complex Tasks

How did we go about developing the preceding checklists? First of all, we gave the matter a lot of thought—something that you, as a person with ADD, must learn to do—and we set aside time to think. Second, we took a brief holiday from the task—a break—and came back to it once again to think some more. Third, we tried the checklists out in real time. Did they work? Had we forgotten something? Finally, we asked ourselves if we had covered everything involved in planning a trip.

Putting Ideas into Practice

We also practiced again and again, breaking down large tasks into small parts or steps. This is something a person with ADD has some difficulty doing. As an exercise, try breaking down into steps such tasks as driving a car or accessing the Internet.

A Routine for Breaking a Complex Task into Small Parts or Steps

Take several days to think about how to break down the task, or ask your ADD coach to help you do this.

- Brainstorm. Think of the various parts of the task and all the possible steps needed to complete it.
- Sleep on it. Look at your brainstorming ideas a second time. Add and subtract items as needed.

- Put the steps in order. Visualize yourself doing the task to help you order the steps.
- Estimate. Be realistic about the amount of time each step will take; include time to think and make decisions and allow time for things to go wrong.
- Plan ahead. Determine and locate any information you need before you begin.

Giving a Dinner Party

The remainder of this chapter deals with complex tasks that can cause you anxiety because of your organizational difficulties, such as planning a party or giving a presentation at work. It is true that some of the anxiety inherent in both of these undertakings can be caused by extreme shyness or poor self-esteem; once again, these are types of issues that need to be discussed with a therapist. Notwithstanding the extremes, far too many capable people with ADD procrastinate because of organizational issues.

You can probably give yourself a host of reasons to put off having a party: your place is too messy; you are too busy; you can't cook. Just contemplating giving a party may make you feel so overwhelmed that you wouldn't know where to begin. It seems that so many little details have to be attended to and the responsibility of entertaining people for several hours is scary. You are afraid your party will be a flop—and thus, you will be a flop. You know, of course, that this catastrophic thinking is far from the truth. So, if you really want to have a party but are still afraid to take the plunge, try using the checklists and routines (see "Barbara's Dinner Paty" on pages 114 and 115) presented here to help you organize yourself, remove some of the responsibility from your shoulders, and overcome your anxiety.

Limit Your Responsibilities for the Party

Make your party simple and easy. Instead of cooking everything from scratch, buy ready-made items such as salad dressing or veggie dip. You can buy wonderful desserts at a good bakery and save yourself a lot of time.

If cooking everything yourself makes you anxious, you can invite people for a potluck. In this way, your primary responsibility will be getting your house ready. The guests will be responsible for the food. Even if you aren't planning a potluck, some of your friends may volunteer to make something. Let them! This means less responsibility for you. As another way of limiting your responsibilities and lessening your anxiety, you could invite guests just for dessert after the movies or for refreshments before the theater.

If having your home presentable is giving you anxiety, remember that only the public rooms need to be presentable. You can close the door on your messy study, bedroom, or private bath, if the guests won't be using them.

Try to invite at least one or two outgoing, fun-loving people who will be able to entertain the others when you are busy. You can also ask a close friend to act as an informal assistant host.

Revise your standards. Remember that neither you nor the party must be perfect. The house doesn't have to be completely clean. You don't have to do everything yourself—from square one.

A Checklist to See What Makes a Good Party

Think of all the parties you have attended. What did you like best about them? Check off the three qualities that you liked the most:

- ❏ The house was clean.
- ❏ The food was delicious.
- ❏ The host was brilliant.
- ❏ The conversation was interesting.
- ❏ The food was served exactly on time.
- ❏ I laughed a lot.
- ❏ Everything was coordinated so well (e.g., all the dishes matched).
- ❏ I met a lot of new people.

■ Barbara's Dinner Party

Barbara uses several lists to help her prepare for a party, including an itemized menu, a shopping list, and a schedule.

Barbara's Menu

Before dinner:	Drinks, appetizers (cheese and crackers, nuts, veggies and dip)
Dinner:	Salad
	Bread and rolls, butter
	Flank steak, roast potatoes, asparagus
Dessert:	Blueberry pie, ice cream
	Coffee, tea

Barbara's Shopping Checklist

Wine	Crackers	Coffee
Beer	Cheese	Tea
Soda	Nuts	Sugar
Juice	Lemons, olives	Cream
Dip	Carrots, celery	Cucumbers
Lettuce, spinach	Tomatoes	Salad dressing
Butter	Bread and rolls	Napkins
Flank steak	Potatoes	Asparagus
Olive oil	Salt and pepper	Garlic powder
Blueberries	Piecrust mix	Charcoal
Onion	Garlic	Rosemary

Barbara's Countdown for the Day of the Party

Guest arrival time 6:30 P.M.
Dinner to be served around 7:15 P.M.
Day of party
1:00   Make dessert.
2:00   Straighten house.

3:00	Set table.
3:15	Make salad.
3:30	Rest.
4:00	Set out drinks: wine, beer, soda, juice, lemon, olives, glasses.
4:15	Set up appetizers: cheese/crackers, veggies/dip, nuts.
4:45	Fry onion and garlic in olive oil.
5:15	Cut up potatoes and mix in pan with fried onion.
5:30	Start fire on grill and preheat oven.
5:45	Get dressed.
6:20	Put potatoes in oven.
6:30	Guests arrive. Offer them appetizers and something to drink.
6:45	Put asparagus in oven (olive oil, rosemary).
6:50	Put flank steak on grill (garlic powder, black pepper).
7:00	Put bread in oven, turn flank steak on grill.
7:15	Remove bread; remove flank steak, potatoes, asparagus. Call the guests to sit down.

❏ Everyone pitched in to help (e.g., I helped clear the table after dinner).

❏ I learned a lot.

❏ Other.

Look at the aspects that you checked. That is what you want your own party to be like. Now when you plan your party, visualize what you want it to be like based on these preferences.

Planning for the Party

Planning the party begins with self-talk and visualization and continues with lists, lists, and more lists.

Tell yourself:
- Relax and stay calm.
- Enjoy yourself. If you're having fun, everyone else will also.
- You are not launching a spaceship. Everything doesn't have to be perfect.
- You are just a facilitator. Most parties take care of themselves.
- Mistakes might happen. Be the first to laugh at them.
- It's OK if things do not work out exactly as planned.
- You can ask your guests to help you.

Visualize:
- What your party will be like
- How relaxed you will look and feel at the party
- How easily you will handle problems should they occur
- How happy everyone will look

Make lists:
- Guests
- Menu
- Shopping
- Countdown
- What you will wear (try clothes on a week before)
- Items that need to be borrowed, such as chairs, tables, and serving pieces
- Guest towels in the bathroom, place to put coats

From the time your guests begin arriving to the time you sit them down to eat, you will be welcoming people, introducing them to each other, and paying attention to the dinner as it is cooking. If you choose a main course that can be cooked beforehand, such as a stew or casserole, you can leave yourself free to socialize with guests until it's time to serve the dinner. Then again, preparing parts of the dinner while guests are milling around can be a good thing, as it encourages a natural type of conversation that can keep you from feeling nervous.

Making a Presentation at Work

It may be hard to think of making a presentation at work as similar to giving a dinner party, but they do have several common aspects. In both situations, you are the one in charge, it is not clear what the finished product will look like, it's hard to figure out where to start or what to include, and a certain amount of organization is required for optimal efficiency. In addition, in your zeal to make things perfect, you may try to create something that is not really you.

Any and all of these elements can make a person with ADD anxious—a major reason you procrastinate. You put off planning the presentation because you either don't know where to start, are not sure of how much material to cover or how to organize it, underestimate the amount of time it takes to prepare for the presentation, or are afraid of performing in public.

Performance anxiety can be overcome to some extent with self-talk and visualization: you keep encouraging yourself with self-talk, and you visualize yourself making an interesting presentation—smiling and looking confident and relaxed. A ground rule is that you should present only on topics in which you are interested and about which you know a lot. Remember that there is no one way to make a presentation; be sure to take into account your own style and personality. Also keep in mind that it isn't necessary to have an answer to all questions. You can say, "I don't know" or "I'll check." Finally, don't try to cram too much information into the presentation. People need time to digest what you are saying.

The following tips can make you feel more relaxed and help make your presentations more interesting:

- Plan to use slides or overheads. Using visual aids can save you from having to memorize or read your comments. The points you've written on your slides or overheads will trigger information that you want to get across to the audience.
- Familiarize yourself with the functions of electronic tools you will be using. Know how to work any slide projector, laptop

program, slide carousel, pointer, or other item that is part of your session.

- Think carefully about what you will wear. Wear clothing that is comfortable and makes you feel good. Dressing for success leads to greater confidence.
- Assume you will begin your presentation five to ten minutes late. Allow time for your audience to arrive and settle down. (But don't wait too long for the latecomers, because your audience will get restless.)
- Don't drink coffee or tea right before your presentation. Coffee and tea can make your mouth dry. Drink water instead.
- Try to "read" your audience. Look at individual members of the audience for their responses, and modify what you are saying so they will understand it.
- Invite the audience to ask questions. Questions help focus you on information the audience wants. They also make people listen more attentively to what you are saying.
- Maintain control over the length of questions and answers. Answer questions only if they don't digress from the topic. You can say, "Let's discuss that question after the presentation."
- Check the time occasionally during your presentation. Be prepared to speed up or omit something if you are running out of time.

Checklist for Developing a Presentation

When developing your presentation, choose the title carefully. It should clearly describe the topic and set audience expectations. Don't get too "cute."

Identify the target audience, including their backgrounds and interests. Ask yourself: What does the audience want to know? What questions do they have? Identify the questions that you feel comfortable answering.

Pay special attention to your opening remarks and to your summary and closing remarks. Always incorporate examples in your presentation, either with personal stories or with jokes, as appropriate. This helps with pacing as well as increasing the audience's understanding.

Be sure to include time for questions and answers, either at the end or during your presentation. Questions from the audience can spark your own interest and tap into any ideas you may have forgotten.

The following checklist should also help you as you prepare and organize materials for your next presentation:

❑ Prepare overheads or slides (use a size 20 to 24 font, in boldface, with extra space between lines).

❑ Number overheads or slides.

❑ Insert blank sheets of paper between overheads to write notes to yourself.

❑ Prepare handouts. Include a cover page with your name, date, title of presentation, conference sponsor, and city and state so people can contact you. Number each page.

❑ Duplicate handouts yourself or send them to the sponsoring agency to have them duplicated. (Send them at least one month in advance.)

❑ Record slide presentation on floppy disk, CD, or memory stick.

A Day-of-the-Presentation Checklist

On the day of the presentation, you can use the following checklists or develop your own based on these suggestions.

One hour before the presentation or when you arrive at the site:
❑ Check in at the conference.

❑ Check the time and room number of your presentation.

Forty-five minutes before the presentation:
❑ Locate the room.

❑ Locate the nearest restroom.

❑ Check all equipment and supplies that you'll need—which may include the screen, slide projector bulb, table for your materials, water and drinking glasses, arrangement of the room, electric outlets, light switches, microphones, laptop, projectors, and extension cords.

Fifteen to thirty minutes before the presentation:

❑ Freshen up in the restroom.

The Satisfaction of Getting Things Done

The key to planning is to recognize what a wonderful difference it will make in your life. Not only will you eliminate a great deal of stress and anxiety, but also you will be able to add enjoyment to your life by entertaining people in your own home. In addition, you will be able to take advantage of opportunities at work that you had been afraid to tackle, such as traveling to another city to make a presentation on something of note that you've been doing.

Staying in charge of your distractibility is a must. Careful planning, including a liberal amount of thinking time, will allow you to organize even the most chaotic life. Finally, using the strategies and checklists in this chapter, and developing your own, will help ensure that you complete the tasks for which you are responsible efficiently and effectively.

8

People Get Irritated with Me and I Don't Know Why

MARSHALL RECENTLY MARRIED *a widow with three children. He displayed a level of warmth and caring toward them that they hadn't experienced in years. In the first few months, the family flourished. Marshall was supportive of his wife's high-powered job. She brought a sense of order and stability to his life. But, although Marshall and the children thrived, his wife soon began to feel overburdened and resentful of the chaos and clutter that Marshall brought to the relationship. Marshall has ADD. Cleaning up after him is a full-time job. He leaves his clothes strewn throughout the house, expecting her to pick them up and put them away—even the kids don't do that. He leaves his tools all over the house and can't find them when he needs them. He loses his keys, and after borrowing hers, he loses those, too. Whenever he makes a snack for himself, he manages to make the kitchen look as if a family of twelve has just eaten a holiday meal. Marshall's wife has found herself turning into a shrew. Reminding him to put his things away* has turned into yelling at him for making her life so difficult. Marshall is hurt when his wife becomes so angry at him. He says that he tries to do the right thing but always seems to fail. All the love on which this family was founded is now being eaten away.

Jeannie and her son have similar problems. Jeannie, who also has ADD, is sweet and generally quiet. She's the kind of person who takes cookies and casseroles to her friends to cheer them up when they're sad. You would never know how smart she is by just having a casual conversation with her, as she often seems flaky. Yet, she has a master's degree in microbiology and secretly desires to get her Ph.D. someday. Her youngest boy, Adam, age nine, is having a tough time in school because he is often late and misses almost a half hour of class every morning. He tries to make up the work, because the teacher insists that he do so, but often he cannot. On those occasions, the teacher makes him stay in during recess to catch up. Adam rebels against this treatment and frequently ends up in detention. Jeannie, for her part, has a hard time getting up in the morning and getting started on her day. She insists on driving Adam to school because she worries about his crossing the busy intersection in front of the school. Jeannie and Adam have terrible fights in the morning—not because Adam takes so much time getting ready, but because Jeannie does. Actually, Adam gets angry with his mother quite often: when she forgets to pack his lunch, when he doesn't have a clean pair of pants to wear, or when she neglects to sign his permission slip for the school trip. Jeannie, who loves her son dearly, is in danger of totally alienating him.

By some people's standards, Phil has it all: brains, money, a handsome family, a fine home. He also has ADD. Yes, Phil is bright enough, but he is often impatient and tactless. He is insensitive to others' feelings and says he can't be bothered wondering how someone will take something he says. He knows a lot about a lot of topics and feels free to dominate any and all conversations. Many people find him obnoxious and try to avoid him. Others, attracted by his interesting and unique ideas, stay around for a while and then leave—unable to tolerate the constant insults and lack of *respect. Phil tries to rationalize some of the remarks directed toward him by angry coworkers and others, saying, "She's overly sensitive," or "I couldn't help it—what he said was so stupid." In truth, though, other people's remarks do hurt him. He is becoming aware that people often try to avoid him. He is becoming depressed because he realizes that he has no friends.*

As you can see, the relationships Marshall, Jeannie, and Phil have with other people are being negatively affected by their ADD. Each of the three has many good qualities that others find attractive but that are being overshadowed by impulsivity, distractibility, and disorganization.

ADD can affect any relationship, no matter how much the individuals involved care for each other, and no matter how smart or nice they are. Has someone you love ever said to you, "I can't take this anymore!" while pointing to the shoes and socks you dumped without thinking in the middle of the living room? In this chapter, we hope to help you uncover how ADD is affecting your relationships and suggest some strategies to help you make your life more satisfying.

What Makes Them So Angry

At first, most people find individuals with ADD attractive. They are often described as friendly, fun to be with, and interesting. In other words, generally, you make a good first impression. Lucky you! However, people with ADD—these usually decent, caring individuals—often, without intending to do so, make other people very angry. How can this be?

When you are always late to appointments, when you repeatedly fail to follow through on promises, when you inadvertently insult your coworker for the fifth time, when you continually leave your shoes and socks in the middle of the living room floor where someone could trip over them, you reach a point at which people turn on you. You have finally made them very angry. They get angry because of something you said or did—not once, but many times over many months. It's over the long haul that people with ADD may become difficult to live with.

Many people with ADD are not great communicators. One reason is that their thoughts often fly much faster than their words, so their ideas seem sketchy, and their descriptions and directions seem incomplete. In addition, because their minds wander, they lose track of what they are saying. A third reason is that because they often speak impulsively, their comments can seem tactless and insulting. They often blurt out things that are best left unsaid. Finally, they may not remember what you or they just said five minutes ago!

Problems with focusing and maintaining attention also get in the way of listening to what someone is saying and responding appropriately. These problems, taken together, do not make for satisfying conversations! In addition, people with ADD flit from one unfinished task to another, leaving messes wherever they go. Because of their difficulty in maintaining attention and avoiding distractions, they can be insensitive to the needs of others. They may not be able to "read" other people's feelings. They do not pick up on the behavioral cues others give to indicate the beginnings of negative feelings (frowning, tensing, shaking the head, turning away, etc.) and proceed blithely with what they were saying or doing, until an explosion erupts.

In short, in the daily give and take of love and friendship, people with ADD are often sorely remiss. Yet, they are frustrated and hurt when others react angrily to what they say or do. Because others seem to misunderstand them, get angry, or withdraw, their feelings of self-worth plummet. They often feel depressed.

Remember, You Are Not a Bad Person

It is important for you to understand that although ADD can cause you to act inconsiderately, you are not basically inconsiderate. You bring many positive qualities to a relationship that others will value and seek out. The goal is to "correct" some ADD-caused behaviors so that others can see you for who you really are: a caring, considerate, dependable, and interesting person.

You also need to keep in mind that you are not the only one responsible for a particular relationship. It takes two to tango, as the saying goes. Each person in a friendship or relationship has responsibility for making it work. If you want to try to "fix" a relationship, both parties need to talk things through and/or seek help or counseling. A psychiatrist, psychologist, or social worker can be of great help to you in forming and keeping satisfying relationships and friendships.

Why Should You Care About Other People's Feelings?

You are probably shocked to find out that others think of you as inconsiderate. Few people set out to deliberately hurt someone. You do care about others' feelings, but you need to learn how to manage your impulsivity and distractibility so that these traits don't interfere with your relationships as much.

People like Phil, who have difficulty reading other people's feelings, often wonder why they should care in the first place. Aren't people responsible for controlling their own feelings? Shouldn't Phil be able to say anything he wants to? Isn't the information Phil wants to impart the most important thing? Why is everyone getting so bent out of shape?

Two parties are involved in an exchange of information: the speaker and the receiver. If you identify with Phil's situation, you need to learn how to express yourself in a way that people are willing to accept. Unless you learn to speak appropriately and respectfully, the message you deliver will not be understood, believed, accepted, or acted on by the other person. You need to carefully monitor what you say and the way you say it if you want the listener to do any of the following in response:

- Cooperate or help
- Agree with you
- Take your advice

If you want to get people to like you, you must learn how to be kind and considerate when interacting with others. If you're like Phil, you also need to learn to talk less and to really listen when someone else wants to talk. You will have to teach yourself to remove such words as *stupid* and *boring* from your vocabulary and learn how to respect the way other people think and feel. You must also learn how to rein in your impulsivity.

And finally, you will have to learn how to read the cues others are sending as to their feelings about what you are saying or doing.

How to Read Cues from Other People

Short of being hit on the head, it is often difficult for people with ADD to tell if someone is angered or hurt by something they said or did. Again, this failure can be caused by not paying attention to or recognizing the subtle cues another person is giving, or it may be a disorder in and of itself. These subtle cues can be changes in the person's tone of voice, facial expression, or body stance. Nonverbal cues such as these can be as telling as verbal messages.

Recognizing cues to the positive feelings of others is relatively easy. Positive cues include the following:

- Smiling, laughing
- Hugging, touching
- Clapping, giving thumbs-up, opening the arms
- Relaxing the body
- Nodding
- Calling others to listen in
- Expressing praise

Subtle Negative Cues

Cues to others' negative feelings can be much more subtle, for a variety of reasons. People tend to be indirect when you do or say something they don't like. For example, a supervisor who is trying to correct you might say, "Why don't you try to do it this way?" This may sound as if you could do it the supervisor's way or continue doing it your way, but it actually means "Stop doing it your way."

Use the following list to help you pick up on some subtle negative cues. Visualize a tense or uncomfortable situation that you recently witnessed or of which you were a part. Did you notice anyone doing any of the following?

- Edging away or leaning away during the conversation
- Appearing to avoid a particular person (e.g., walking around the corner when the person approached)
- Saying, "OK, let's move on"
- Stop talking, and turning away
- Saying, "You're not listening to me"
- Shaking his or her head no several times, with the mouth turned down
- Smiling (grimly) but saying nothing
- Not responding at all, or looking away, when someone was talking—as if the other person didn't exist
- Looking confused

If you are able to recognize subtle negative cues, you will be able to modify what you are saying or doing so that the other person stops getting angry or hurt and the interchange can proceed more positively.

An Exercise to Help You Recognize Cues

Use this exercise to help you recognize both verbal and nonverbal cues. The next time you start to watch one of your favorite sitcoms or dramas on TV, pay careful attention to one character. As the show progresses (and maybe during a commercial), ask yourself:

- How is the character feeling?
- What cues indicate the character's feelings?
- Why did the character say or do something?

Then try to predict how the character will react:

- What will the person do next?
- What will the person say when another character says or does something?

Check yourself. Were you right? Did you miss something?

If you do get into a situation in which you inadvertently hurt someone or make someone angry, apologize. Tell the person that you must have misspoken and would like to try again to say what you meant without causing hurt.

Talk Less

As noted, people with ADD can be very talkative. This characteristic can be a blessing at a social gathering when a conversation lags and there are long, uncomfortable silences, or when no one else has anything to say. However, people with ADD can talk constantly—about trivial as well as interesting subjects—not allowing anyone else to get a word in edgewise.

Under many circumstances, less talk on your part can promote a relationship. You need to understand that it's OK to have some companionable silences in a conversation. Silence gives people time to think things through. You will be surprised at how wise a friend will think you are after you have listened quietly to a sad story—not saying anything. Many situations call for less talk rather than more. When you encounter such situations, try telling yourself to keep quiet or stop talking. For instance:

- If you think that someone has recently gained weight, the best thing you can do is—say nothing. Censor your urge to suggest the perfect diet or to commiserate by noting that you, too, have gained weight. Say nothing.
- If someone asks your opinion about something, the best thing you can do is answer—clearly but briefly. Don't go on and on to make sure the person understands. Don't move to another subject and explain that too. Stop.
- If someone wants to talk to you about something that has happened, the best thing you can do is listen—quietly. No comments. (You could nod or hug the person, if appropriate.)
- If you make a suggestion to someone and the person rejects it for some reason, stop; don't push it.
- Avoid talking when someone else is talking, thinking, or watching TV.

Listen Better

When a friend or family member asks to talk to you, stop doing whatever you were involved in and tell yourself to listen. Also tell yourself to suppress any distracting thoughts that can interfere with your listening. Listening requires that you exert control over your attention and distractibility by using self-talk. Practice using the following routine while you talk with someone dear to you.

1. Move to a quiet, nondistracting place, if you're having difficulty hearing.
2. Face the speaker.
3. Don't ask unnecessary questions. Ask the speaker to repeat or explain only as necessary for you to understand.
4. Keep reminding yourself to pay attention.
5. Be sure the speaker has finished a thought before you say anything.
6. Make sure you stick to the topic.

When You're at a Meeting

At a meeting, remember that less can be more. It is better to talk less and make a few choice points than to talk a lot and bore or anger people because you are dominating the conversation. It is also important for you to keep your attention focused on what others are saying. Put the following suggestions into practice at your next meeting.

Before the meeting:
- Make yourself a small sign that says Be <u>Q</u>uiet and place it on the table in front of you (where no one else can see it).
- Take a pad of paper and a pen or pencil with you to take notes.

During the meeting:
- Sit up and face the speaker. Slouching makes it easier to daydream.
- Keep reminding yourself to pay attention.

- Practice not saying anything for at least ten minutes. (Try using a prop: put a pencil in your mouth and keep it there throughout the meeting.)
- Take notes about what the speaker is saying, what others say, and about what you want to say. Ask yourself, Did anyone else say the things you wanted to say? Were your points covered by others?
- Listen for signal words such as: "The main reason," "Three important trends," "In conclusion," or "Primarily." (The information that follows these signal words is important for you to focus on and remember.)
- Before asking a question, check your notes to see if the answer has already been given. Ask questions only if you don't understand something—not just to impress someone with how smart you are.

After the meeting:
- Check with a coworker to be sure that you heard the important messages.

Renegotiate Relationships

As we have seen, ADD can have serious effects on relationships, and this is especially true of relationships between couples. Many of these troubled relationships lead to divorce, even in cases in which the spouses still care for each other. In fact, people with ADD have a higher divorce rate than the average. Becoming aware of the effects your ADD can have on your relationship is the first step toward saving the relationship.

One way to become more aware of your partner's interests and obligations is to make a monthly calendar for the two of you. (Look back at Chapter 6 for our sample calendar.) Enter appointments, work responsibilities, and recreational activities for both of you, and discuss them to find out more about them.

We also think that the best way to renegotiate a relationship that you care about is for both of you to see a counselor who is familiar with ADD. The person with ADD may also need to see a coach to help him or her with some ADD-related behavior.

Focus on Your Partner

Both you and your partner can use the next exercise to help you assess the relationship. Many of the qualities listed, both good and bad, are by-products of ADD. People with ADD tend to seek out stability in their partners. Partners without ADD tend to be attracted by the excitement a person with ADD can bring to a relationship. Opposites do attract. Recall Marshall and his wife, whose situation we discussed at the beginning of the chapter. This would be a good exercise for them. Each brings different but valuable assets to the relationship. Each also has specific needs, and there are some incompatibilities that have to be resolved.

Before you and your partner complete the exercise for yourselves, see if you can do it with Marshall and his wife in mind. (You will have to use your imagination at several points.)

Directions: Each person completes the checklist individually. (Remember: the first time, you are Marshall and his wife.) Start by visualizing your partner and asking yourself, "What attracted me to this person in the first place?" Then, read the list of attractive qualities in Table 8.1, and check all that apply; place a star by the most important ones.

Next, visualize the same partner again and ask yourself, "What irritates me most about this person?" Read the list of irritating qualities in Table 8.2, and check all that apply; place a star by the ones that are unacceptable to you.

Then, partners should compare answers and ask one another: Are Marshall and his wife willing to trade off a bad characteristic of the other person for a good characteristic? Can one of them utilize a personal strength of their own to overcome or ignore a weakness in the other? How would you advise them?

Table 8.1 Attractive Qualities

Quality	Yes?	Most Important Quality (*)
Exciting		
Enthusiastic		
Calm		
Organized		
Fun		
Creative		
Loving/caring		
Outgoing/friendly		
Stable		
Sexually fulfilling		
Intellectual		
Dependable		
Sense of humor		
Makes me feel good about myself		
Good work ethic/responsible		
Understanding		
Loyal		
Honest		
Other		

Table 8.2 Irritating Qualities

Quality	Yes?	Unacceptable (*)
Messy		
Impatient		
Inattentive		
Doesn't understand my needs		
Orders me around		
Daydreams too much		
Temperamental		
Depressed		
Lazy		
Irresponsible (explain)		
Withdrawn		
Selfish (explain)		
Drives me crazy (explain)		
Embarrasses me (explain)		
Overly critical		
Compulsively neat		
Controlling/bossy		
Drinks too much		
Other		

Now that you have worked through this exercise for Marshall and his wife, try it for yourself and your partner. Do you see some trade-offs you both can make? Can you renegotiate your relationship to make it more satisfying?

Focus on Your Child

Now let's revisit Jeannie, who also was introduced at the beginning of the chapter. Her ADD has a profound negative effect on her relationship with her son. It's easy to get wrapped up in your own needs and problems and to lose sight of the concerns of the people you hold most dear. Although Jeannie wants to do it all—be a caring friend, be a good mother, have a smoothly running household, get a Ph.D.—she can barely get out of the house in the morning, due to her problems with ADD. At this moment in her life, she has to tell herself that she can't do it all and has to decide what her priorities are. As a single parent, she can easily name her priority: her child.

Since Jeannie's problems with ADD are the reason her son is chronically late for school, she needs to reconsider her choice to drive him to school every day. Is there really a danger in letting him cross the busy intersection in front of the school? Do all the other parents drive their children? Aren't there traffic lights and safety patrols on all the corners? Does Adam want her to drive him? If Jeannie were to let her son walk to school every day, a big problem between them could be eliminated. Adam, who does not have ADD and is a bright boy, could get himself to school on time. Jeannie also needs to tell herself firmly that it is her responsibility to make sure her son has clean clothes to wear to school. That means she will have to wash the clothes at least twice a week. She needs to make sure his lunch is ready for him to take with him when he leaves every day, which means she will have to shop at least once a week to buy what he likes to eat. She can prepare his lunch the night before so that it is ready for him in the morning. If she can focus on her son and his needs, she can eliminate many of the problems between them. Constantly reminding herself to focus on her son may help her overcome some of her ADD-related problems. Nevertheless, though she will feel much happier when she and her son are no longer fighting regularly, it is clear that she still needs some counseling.

If you identify with Jeannie, you first have to rethink why your lifestyle is making your child so stressed and then prioritize and figure out how to change it. Then, the very next thing you have to do is get help for yourself by seeing a counselor. You, like Jeannie, will have to tend to your own fire in order to help someone else.

Follow Through on Commitments

The first trick to following through on commitments is to not overcommit yourself. We talked about overcommitment as a real time waster in Chapter 6. People with ADD often impulsively volunteer for much more than they can deliver. They think they are being good guys—promising to do things others don't want to do. But when they don't follow through, people who were depending on them get annoyed and angry. Use the following tips to help you follow through on your commitments at work:

- Become aware of the extent to which you impulsively volunteer for more than you can handle.
- Before you promise to do something, consider the other jobs in which you're involved. Ask yourself, "Do I have time to finish this proposed project, given my other responsibilities?"
- Ask yourself if you have the skills and information necessary, before you promise to do something.
- Before going into a meeting, tell yourself not to volunteer until you have checked your current commitments. Write a note to yourself that says "Don't raise your hand."
- Don't volunteer or promise to do something just to be nice or to get brownie points.
- Once you commit, write down specifically what you have promised to do and when it needs to be completed.
- Make yourself a time line of all your responsibilities and commitments and when they must be completed.

- If it looks as if you will not be able to finish on time, let others know as soon as possible.
- Don't volunteer the services of someone else unless you first check with the person.
- If your supervisor tells you to do something and you feel you don't have the time, say so. If it is something with a high priority, ask your supervisor if it would be possible to reduce some of your other responsibilities until you complete the high-priority task.

Make a Pledge to Be on Time for Appointments

Most people with ADD are aware that they often are late for appointments or miss them entirely. And of course, they apologize profusely. But after the fourth or fifth apology, the other parties involved start getting rather irritated. Since you are aware that you are often late (awareness is half the battle), you can begin to remedy the situation by making a pledge to be on time from now on. (Again, refer back to Chapter 6 for planning strategies and ways to avoid the time wasters that often make us late.)

Make a Pledge to Pick Up After Yourself

Before pledging to pick up after yourself, you need to become fully aware of your habit of dropping your things all over the house. Moreover, you need to understand (1) how much more work this creates for others and (2) how much it irritates them. Once you have a realistic understanding of the situation, you are ready to begin to follow through on your pledge.

If you tend to be oblivious to the fact that you leave your things around the house, plan to do a routine "sweep" around each "public" room once or twice a day. Tell yourself to look carefully and make sure that nothing of yours is on the floor or on the table that doesn't belong there. You can also do this after you have prepared something for yourself to eat. Refer back to Chapter 5 for additional ways to keep your house organized.

Work to Become More Self-Aware

As discussed in Chapter 2, people with ADD have a particular problem with self-awareness. Again, this is largely due to your distractibility and impulsivity. You don't really listen to yourself speak and don't pay enough attention to the things you do. You often act without thinking. Therefore, it is hard for you to become aware of the things you say or do.

Despite the obstacles, you need to try to figure out what you tend to say or do that hurts or irritates people so that you can stop yourself from doing these inconsiderate things. You can start by trying to keep a log (see Figure 8.1) of situations in which someone got angry or hurt by something you said or did, or situations that ended badly but you didn't know why.

Once again, remember that both people in a relationship share responsibility for the relationship. What you said or did in a particular situation may not have been the cause of the outcome. But if too many situations end badly for you, look for the part you played.

This chapter dealt with some of the most difficult adjustments you can make. Trying to make even minor changes to your communication style or your behavior can be a long, difficult process. That is why you may need the support of a counselor or therapist.

You will also need a great deal of practice before these changes become second nature. You will be substituting good habits for destructive ones. Whatever changes you decide to try, they must feel compatible with who you are as a person. The targets of these changes are the irritating habits caused by ADD that get in the way of satisfying relationships.

Figure 8.1 Sample Log Work Sheet

Date: _____

Situation (where, what, who): _____

_____

_____

Exactly what I said or did: _____

_____

_____

What I meant to say or do: _____

_____

_____

What triggered the situation: _____

_____

_____

What I expected to happen when I said or did this: _____

_____

_____

What happened in reality: _____

_____

_____

What was the consequence? _____

_____

_____

Why did this happen? _____

_____

_____

How could I have changed what I said or did to make this conclusion
more satisfying to me? _____

_____

_____

What did the other person feel about the encounter (if I feel comfortable asking that person)? _____

_____

_____

PART III

Looking Ahead to the Future

9

Medication: Should I? Shouldn't I?

PERCY, A SUCCESSFUL *graphic artist, has ADD. Up till now, his job at the advertising agency had been a good fit for Percy, and his bosses were happy with him. They were so happy, in fact, that they promoted him to a management position two months ago. However, what should have been a cause for celebration has turned into a source of considerable stress for Percy. His ADD severely impedes his ability to master the organizational skills demanded by his new position. Percy has heard about medication for ADD and wonders if it could help him with his problems at work. At the same time, he worries that medication might stifle his spontaneity and creativity. He doesn't know what to do. Even with medication, at some point Percy will have to make another decision: whether to stay on in his new, higher-paying, stressful management post or return to the old job he loved—graphic designer.*

Percy is similar to many adults with ADD who wonder if medication is right for them. Deciding whether to take medication for ADD can be a struggle, for various reasons. People commonly cite the following reservations, among others:

- They believe that they should take medication rarely and only if they are physically sick.
- They believe that they should be able to manage their problems without medication.
- They are afraid they will become addicted.
- They are afraid medication will change their personality.
- They are afraid medication will turn them into zombies.

Some people with ADD say they have tried medication and it didn't work. Others who have tried medication say they didn't like the way they felt on medication. While these objections may be valid, if you tried medication once and were disappointed, that does not mean that you shouldn't try again. Some newer medications have fewer side effects than those with which many people are familiar. Also, the first time you tried medication, you may have been given too low a dose to be effective. A physician who specializes in medication for ADD is more likely than others to prescribe the medication or combination of medications that is best for you and at the optimal dosage.

What Medication Can Do

Medication is not a magic bullet. It cannot "cure" your problems. You cannot rely on medication alone to make things work for you. What medication can give you is a large boost in the direction of your goals. Uri, an inventor, described it this way: "I have all these wonderful ideas flitting through my head all the time. Medication gives me a chance to capture one."

Research suggests that the most effective method of easing the symptoms of ADD is a combination of medication, psychotherapy, and training in the use of compensatory strategies (such as the strategies we have given you in this book). Different medications or combinations of medications can help you directly in controlling the following conditions:

- Inattention
- Distractibility
- Impulsivity

By helping you directly with the symptoms of ADD, medications can also help alleviate some of the secondary problems you might be experiencing, such as irritability, anxiety, and depression. Can you learn to manage many of the problems caused by ADD without medication? Yes, to some extent, but medication can make it much easier.

The Medication Decision

Making the decision regarding whether to take medication should not be done lightly. You need information, about yourself and about the medication. You also need time to make up your mind. The suggestions in this section can aid you in weighing your options.

First, make sure you get a full diagnostic workup, if you haven't gotten one already. This evaluation will help determine whether you have ADD or other problems that can coexist with ADD, and what the problem areas are. You should also get a general physical checkup from your family doctor to determine if you have high blood pressure or any other medical condition that would raise a cautionary flag for some types of medication. You will need to keep a list of all the prescription and non-prescription medications (including vitamin supplements and herbal remedies) you are now taking.

Next, consult a physician who specializes in ADD and the medications used to alleviate symptoms. This is generally a psychiatrist. (To find one in your area, you can contact your general physician or your local chapter of CHADD or ADDA; see the "Resources"section later in this book.) The psychiatrist can explain the benefits of each medication, as well as the undesirable side effects. He or she can also tell you about any possible negative interactions between the suggested ADD drugs and any other medications you are currently taking. You might also want to ask friends who take medication about their experiences.

It is easy to take a trial run of many of the stimulant medications, since they are short acting (four to six hours) and do not need days or weeks to build up in your bloodstream. You can take a week's trial run of stimulant medications and monitor the effects.

Types of Medication

Medications used for ADD fall into four general types, as seen in Table 9.1: (1) stimulant, (2) antidepressant, (3) antihypertensive, and (4) non-stimulant developed specifically to treat ADD.

The stimulants include Ritalin, Concerta, and Adderall. Stimulants like Ritalin have been in use for more than fifty years.

The antidepressants were originally developed to treat depression but were found to be effective in treating some symptoms of ADD as well; they include Wellbutrin and Desipramine. These medications must be taken for two to four weeks before they become effective; for a trial run you will need to take them for several months.

Table 9.1 Medications to Treat ADD

Type of Medication	Generic/Brand Name
Stimulants	Ritalin
	Concerta
	Adderall
Antidepressants	Wellbutrin
	Desipramine
Antihypertensives	Clonidine
	Atenolol
Nonstimulants developed specifically to treat ADD	Strattera

The antihypertensives were developed to treat high blood pressure, but these, too, were found to be useful in treating some of the symptoms of ADD. These medications include Clonidine and Atenolol. These medications should be carefully monitored by your physician the first few weeks, to make sure that your blood pressure and heart rate are in the normal range.

Strattera is the first of the class of nonstimulants to be developed specifically for the treatment of ADD. This medication, too, takes time to build up in your bloodstream.

These medications, of course, do not all work in the same way to alleviate the symptoms of ADD, nor do they all work on the same symptoms. Your physician will help you sort out which medication or combination is right for you.

New medications for ADD reach the market almost every other month. It is important to read all available information before considering these new products.

Monitoring Your Medication

You will need to monitor your medication for both desirable and undesirable effects. You want to be sure that it helps you with your problem symptoms and does not have side effects that you cannot tolerate. Start monitoring from day one, but give whatever medication you are taking time to take effect. You might even start monitoring yourself several weeks before you begin taking the medication, to get a baseline. Monitor stimulants for at least one week. *Remember that some of the other medications will take weeks to become effective.*

Positive Effects of Medication

You can use this checklist to help you recognize and monitor the positive effects of your medication:

- You feel more alert throughout the day.
- You are able to stay more focused throughout the day.

- You feel more calm when faced with a problem.
- You seem to be getting more work done.
- You are better able to tune out distractions.
- You feel generally less irritable.
- You seem to be able to manage time better.
- You feel "smarter."
- You feel more in control.
- You seem to be better able to focus on and remember what people say.

Negative Effects of Medication

All of the medications cited can have negative side effects. Most are rare; nevertheless, some can be serious enough to require immediate attention. Serious side effects include swelling or hives (allergies); if you experience either of these, call your doctor right away. Other side effects that may be serious include dizziness, confusion, and increased anxiety. Again, report any of these to your physician as soon as you become aware of the condition. Here's a companion list of negative side effects that you need to monitor:

- Swelling or hives
- Cramps
- Nausea or vomiting
- Dizziness
- Sleepiness, fatigue
- Constipation
- Dry mouth
- Insomnia
- Increased irritability, anxiety
- Confusion
- Tics

Some side effects will go away in a week or so, while others will persist. Over-the-counter remedies can be taken to help with some of the conditions, such as constipation, insomnia, and dry mouth. In all cases, you must talk to your physician about any negative side effects that you experience. The physician may then change your medication to one with a reduced level of side effects.

Guidelines for Taking Medication

Keep the following guidelines in mind if you decide to take medication for your ADD:

- Be sure to check on possible interactions between your medication for ADD and any other medications you are taking.
- Call your physician immediately if you have an allergic reaction.
- Take medication only in the dosage prescribed.
- Don't take someone else's medication or give your medication to another person to use.
- Never stop taking any of the antidepressants or antihypertensives suddenly. This can be dangerous.
- Don't stop taking medication without discussing it first with your physician.
- Avoid alcohol.
- Be sure to monitor both your positive and negative side effects. Keep a notebook in which to record any changes (both good and bad) that you notice.

Strategies for Keeping Track of Your Medication

People with ADD are often as disorganized about taking their medication as they are about other facets of their lives. It is not uncommon to find pill bottles and individual pills all over the house of a person with ADD. Pills drop out of pants pockets, wallets, change purses, gloves, and hands. It is also not uncommon to find people with ADD in a panic state because they can't find their medication or are not sure whether they have already taken it. If you're ever not sure if you have taken a pill, it is best not to take another until the next scheduled dose, to guard against an overdose.

Better yet, don't let these things happen to you! You need to develop strategies and routines that facilitate your taking your medication at the prescribed times. Here are some suggestions:

- Buy a pillbox with compartments for each day of the week (or month). On Sunday of each week, place your daily dose in each compartment. Using this type of pillbox will help ensure that you take the proper dosage each day.
- Keep an extra supply of pills at work, in case you forget to take them at home.
- Always keep your medication in the same location, at home and at work, to prevent misplacing it.
- You can keep medication that you take in the morning near the coffeepot (if you are a morning coffee drinker) and the medication you take at night on a table next to your bed.
- To help you remember to take your medication, pair taking your medication with another habit or routine (e.g., right after you brush your teeth or with your morning beverage).
- Take a moment to feel the medication in your mouth. Is it round, oval, a capsule, rough, smooth? The feel of the medication in your mouth can help you remember whether or not you have taken it.
- Directly after you have taken your medication, say to yourself, "Stop. Put the medication back where it belongs." This will also help to prevent loss.

Reevaluating Medication

You will need to check your medication at least once or twice a year with your physician or therapist. You cannot assume that the type and dose of medication that are working well for you currently will continue to do so. This is true largely because your life experiences change. For example, the amount of medication that is effective for you can vary seasonally due to any summertime allergies you might have or to seasonal affective disorder (SAD), depression caused by the lack of sunshine during the fall and winter. A serious illness or major job setback can require you to reevaluate your medication. Increased responsibility at home or work may also upset the balance you have achieved with your current dose of medication. Be open to change and be sure to reevaluate your options.

Remember that before beginning any course of medication, you need to have a thorough medical and psychological workup to determine if you really have ADD and if there are any contraindications to taking any of the medications. Then ask for a trial period to see if the medication helps you (and if it affects your creativity). Finally, locate a coach (see the "Resources" section at the back of the book) who can work with you while you are on medication to help you manage some of your organizational problems at home or on the job.

10

Making Decisions and Setting Goals

"Decisions, decisions, decisions," *said Diane. "Wherever I go, I have to make decisions. It's bad enough I have to decide whether my kid should start kindergarten this year and whether my car can make it through another winter. Every day, I go into the restaurant to order lunch. And, you know, they have ten sandwiches on the menu, and all of them sound good. So, it takes me ten minutes to decide on a sandwich. I go place my order, and the waitress writes it down, and then she says, 'White, whole wheat, rye, pumpernickel, seven grain, or croissant?' It's driving me crazy. I can't make up my mind when I have so many choices."*

Harry had been working at the same job for thirty years. As a cost-cutting measure, the company was offering thirty-year employees $20,000 as an incentive to retire early. Harry was tempted. But it was an agonizing decision, as he was only fifty-two years old. He felt overwhelmed. He kept putting it off and putting it off. Finally the deadline arrived. Harry had to make a choice that day. He still didn't know what to do. And so the deadline passed.

Harry didn't make a decision, but in a way, he did. By not filing by the deadline, Harry essentially decided not to retire.

We live in a world that requires us to make multiple decisions every day. You go to the supermarket and have to choose from fifteen types of canned soup or from a full aisle of different kinds of cereals. You are faced with toothpaste that fights cavities, controls tartar buildup, or whitens your teeth. And the flavors! No wonder it sometimes takes people with ADD hours to shop for food and household items. To make matters worse, these decisions are relatively trivial compared with some of the life-altering choices most of us have to make at one time or another, having to do with whether to marry, where to live, and, in some cases, whether to take early retirement.

How ADD Affects Decision Making and Goal Setting

Harry and Diane, like many other people with ADD, are bad at making decisions and often make bad decisions. Diane says that even selecting a DVD to rent can be agony for her. And how she'll ever decide what to do about her child's education is beyond her. Harry has been working at a dead-end job for three decades, unable to seize the opportunities that have come his way, because he wasn't prepared to take them. He had never upgraded his skills, although he often, halfheartedly, thought about doing so. He couldn't even imagine himself with a better job.

Making decisions and setting goals can be very hard for people with ADD. The difficulties they have with attention are only part of the cause. The major impediment is their problem with organization and planning—the precise skills that are necessary for both making decisions and setting goals. People with ADD often react in the following ways:

- Feel overwhelmed when faced with a problem
- Procrastinate and put off solving problems or making decisions until it is too late

- Use a random, hit-or-miss approach to problem solving
- Don't collect the information necessary to make a decision
- Don't consider all possible solutions
- Lack the patience to develop a plan
- Struggle to manage their attention long enough to solve a problem
- Impulsively go with the first thing that comes to mind

In addition, when it comes to setting goals for themselves, people with ADD often feel overburdened at the thought of planning for the future and unable to project themselves beyond the present. They also have low aspirations, which discourages them from even considering goals. These people have not yet developed a set of skills that can help them make decisions and set goals in a systematic way.

Skills Required for Effective Decision Making and Goal Setting

Making decisions and setting goals require many of the same skills. The most basic of these are self-management skills, which include the ability to restrain impulsivity, focus and maintain attention, and maintain motivation to complete a task.

Here are other skills that are also necessary for effective decision making and goal setting:

- Breaking down the decision or goal into steps or tasks
- Setting a deadline
- Making a plan
- Locating necessary information
- Anticipating problems and pitfalls
- Considering several alternatives and projecting the success of each
- Taking into account one's strengths and weaknesses
- Looking back and analyzing how well the plan worked

This list may seem daunting, but you have already practiced many of these skills if you have completed the other chapters in this book.

Using the Right Tools and a Systematic Approach

If you use a systematic approach to solving problems and making decisions, your solutions and decisions will be more effective, and you'll be able to implement them in the appropriate time frame. When you approach goal setting systematically, you significantly improve your chances of reaching your target. The basic tools that you have used throughout this book—self-talk, visualizing, routines, and the Stop! technique—will help you develop a systematic approach.

Self-talk can continue to bolster your efforts in self-management. Reminders—such as telling yourself, "Stop! Make a plan."—can prompt you to call on some of your other newly acquired skills. To help you set goals that are realistic, ask yourself, "Is this plan too ambitious?" When you start to stray from a task you have assigned yourself, tell yourself, "Stop. Pay attention."

Visualizing is particularly useful for goal setting. You can visualize what the goal will look like, how you will feel when you have attained it, and the steps leading up to it. Visualizing the goal is a great motivator to keep you on course. By the same token, when you're seeking a solution to a problem or considering choices, visualizing each potential solution can steer you to the best answer for you.

You already use routines to help avoid the need for constant decision making. For instance, you take the same route from home to work. (You don't need to ask yourself, "Should I turn left or right?") Some people eat the same breakfast (e.g., coffee and a bagel) every day of the workweek or order the same one or two lunches at their favorite restaurant or fast-food joint. (This is a good suggestion for Diane.) You can easily develop your own routines for the relatively minor decisions you have to make daily. Establishing routines for weightier or more far-reaching decisions and for goal setting isn't always as straightforward. For that reason, it is best done in conjunction with the charts, checklists, and diagrams in the following sections.

Setting Deadlines

When you're solving a problem or making a decision, doing it within the appropriate time frame matters almost as much as the actual decision or solution. If you are a procrastinator and often delay making decisions until it is too late, the first thing you need to do (after clarifying the problem) is to set a deadline for reaching the solution or decision. (Use the time-management skills you developed in Chapter 6.)

When faced with a problem, you should routinely ask yourself, "When must this problem be solved?" or "When must this decision be made?" Similarly, when setting a goal for yourself, you should include the date you want the goal to be attained. You will need to break up your goal or decision into steps and then set up a time line for yourself. This will also help you stay on track until you get there.

Gathering Information

A mistake that many people with ADD make is not getting enough information before trying to solve a problem or make a decision. You often lack the expertise to make a decision on your own. For example, if you are trying to make a decision about whether to have an operation, you need to find out the answers to such questions as these:

- Why is the operation necessary?
- What would happen to me if I didn't have the operation?
- How will I feel after the operation?
- What could go wrong during the operation?

You can get information from your surgeon, a respected medical site on the Internet, and medical journals. You also can and should get a second opinion from another physician.

Or, if your young son or daughter asks your permission to visit a friend, you will need answers to such questions as these:

- Does my child have homework to do?
- Is it too late for my child to go out?

- How far away does the friend live, and how will my child get there and back?
- Will a parent be home to supervise?

If you have a problem at work, you can ask a trusted coworker to help you clearly define the problem, determine what might have caused it, and identify which supervisor might be in a position to help you solve it. If you face the same problem over and over, you may need to get expert advice from the human resources department.

You will also need to gather information when you set goals for yourself, in order to be assured that the goals are realistic and attainable. The type of information needed depends on the specific goal. For example, if you plan on going back to school for a degree or certification, you may need answers to questions such as these:

- How do I apply for admission to the particular program?
- What qualifications must I have for acceptance?
- What courses do I need to take?
- Can I afford the tuition?
- Do I have the time to devote to course work?

Problem-Solving Checklist

Solving problems is often a necessary first step toward making decisions. This next checklist, which is divided into six parts, can help you define a problem, make a plan, come up with possible solutions, follow through on the plan, and adjust it, if necessary. Depending on the specific problem at hand, some of the steps will have to be adapted, some steps can be skipped, and other steps may need to be added.

Define the problem:
❑ What is the problem?
❑ Are there other, related problems?

❏ When and how often does the problem occur?

❏ What evidence is there that a problem exists?

❏ What is the most likely cause of the problem?

❏ Why is it necessary or desirable to solve this problem?

Set a deadline:

❏ Set a range of dates.

❏ Schedule the deadline on your calendar.

Gather information:

❏ Locate the necessary information and make notes.

❏ Make sure the information comes from respected sources.

❏ Gather evidence and examples.

Develop solutions:

❏ Put on your creativity hat. Schedule thinking time.

❏ Over the next several days, brainstorm all possible solutions.

❏ Visualize what each solution would look like.

❏ Use charts and diagrams.

❏ For each prospective solution, list the pros and cons and the possible effects or results.

❏ Select the solution(s) most likely to succeed.

Make a plan:

❏ Visualize yourself performing the various tasks involved in the selected solution.

❏ List the sequence of tasks or steps leading to the solution.

❏ Make a time line, as needed.

❏ Ask yourself, "Is this realistic?"

❏ Schedule (on a calendar) time each week to work on the problem, as needed.

▪ How Diane Made an Important Decision

Diane needed to decide if she should enroll her son, Nathan, in kindergarten this year. In order to figure this out, she used our problem-solving checklist.

Define the problem:

- The results of the kindergarten screening test indicate that although Nathan is quite bright, he has behavior problems and may not be ready to start kindergarten this year.
- Nathan will be five on September 15. The kindergarten cutoff is September 13.
- Nathan wants to go to kindergarten with all his friends.

Set a deadline:

- School starts on September 3. Kindergarten Roundup is set for the week of June 1.
- It is now April.
- Set mid-May for my deadline so I will have time to explain things to Nathan before Kindergarten Roundup.

continued

Monitor and adjust:

- ❏ Check off each task as you complete it.
- ❏ Add tasks if you need to.
- ❏ Locate any additional information that you need.
- ❏ Identify any questions, concerns, or trouble spots, and examine setbacks.
- ❏ Brainstorm possible remedies and their potential effects.
- ❏ Select a course with the best chance of success.
- ❏ Adjust your plan as needed.

Personalize your checklist as much as possible. Refer to yourself as "I." Identify by name any other people who are involved. Specify places

Gather information:
- Ask people who know Nathan for advice (his day care provider, Sunday school teacher, and pediatrician).
- Talk to the kindergarten teacher about what difficulties Nathan might face if he were to enter kindergarten this year.

Develop solutions:
- Keep Nathan in day care this year, and if he seems to be doing well, transfer him to kindergarten in midyear. (Ask the kindergarten teacher if this is feasible.)
- Keep him in day care all year and move him directly to first grade next year, skipping kindergarten entirely.
- Send Nathan to kindergarten this year, and if he seems to be struggling, pull him out in midyear or let him finish the year and hold him back from first grade next year.
- Send Nathan to kindergarten this year. If his problems don't get better, ask the school if Nathan can get extra help.

Make a plan:
- I will base my decision on the advice of the "experts" I have turned to, while taking into account Nathan's wishes.

and situations. For example, Diane would say in describing her problem, "I need to decide whether Nathan should start kindergarten at Jones Elementary this year or whether to wait till next year. Harry might say, "I need to call Kay in Human Resources to find out what my pension would be if I retired next month."

Usually, a problem has more than one possible solution. In fact, you should routinely try to think of at least two solutions to any problem. If you're lucky, you will have several good options from which to choose. However, occasionally you will have to select from a short list of not-so-good alternatives. In those cases, you will have to bite the bullet and choose the least aversive solution. The problem you are facing may have multiple causes, each requiring its own strategic solution.

Decision-Making Checklist

The decision-making checklist is similar to the problem-solving checklist. It includes setting aside thinking time, clearly stating the decision to be made, setting deadlines, gathering information, visualizing each possible decision and its ramifications, using charts and diagrams, factoring your strengths and weaknesses into the equation, and, finally, choosing the most logical decision—one that you can live with.

Diagrams to Help You Solve Problems and Make Decisions

Diagrams help you visualize the causes of a problem, as well as the steps needed to solve a problem or to make a decision. Diagrams can also help you try out possible solutions and choose which you think will be the most effective.

Fishbone Diagram

A "fishbone" diagram helps you isolate and specify multiple causes of a problem and then develop strategies to address each one. For example, Josh, who has ADD, was assigned a new project at work and couldn't get off the starting block. He wasn't sure if this inaction was because of his ADD or other factors. After devoting some time to thinking about the problem, he came up with four possible causes. He realized that he didn't quite understand what was expected of him, he didn't feel that he had the expertise to do the job, the job really didn't interest him, and he actually had a hard time remembering his supervisor's instructions. Josh plotted a fishbone diagram to give himself a better perspective (see Figure 10.1).

Seeing the situation diagrammed this way helped Josh direct his thoughts toward how to deal with the causes of the problem: He could

Figure 10.1 Josh's Fishbone Diagram

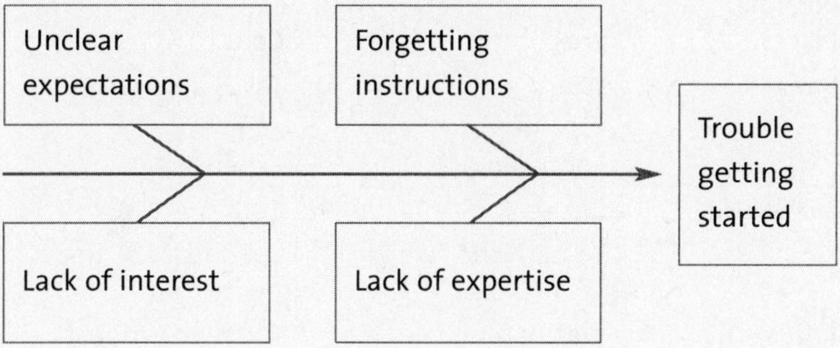

ask his supervisor to go over what was expected—and take written notes so he would remember it. He could locate someone with more experience to help him with the job, and he could use self-talk to keep him focused while he was working. He could also promise himself a reward when he was finished.

Pro/Con Chart

A pro/con chart can help you decide which potential solution has the most merit, by examining the good points and bad points of each option. It can also help you decide whether to take any action at all, by helping you clarify the likely consequences of various approaches. Marge, for example, was planning her vacation and couldn't make up her mind where to go. Using a pro/con chart enabled her to better compare her destination possibilities (see Figure 10.2). After completing her chart, Marge decided to go to Arizona.

Balance of Consequences Work Sheet

A balance of consequences work sheet is another decision-making aid. It provides an organized way to list alternative choices, each with its positive and negative aspects. For example, Walter was in a quandary at work.

Figure 10.2 Marge's Pro/Con Chart

Possible Places	Pros	Cons
Hawaii	Warm	Takes a long time to travel
	Snorkeling	Expensive
Connecticut	Cheap	Cool
	Be with the family	Spend all the time with family
Arizona	Warm	Too many tourists
	Not too expensive	
	See the Grand Canyon	

His supervisor had called him in and expressed concern about the amount of unfinished work on his desk. The supervisor stressed that Walter was a very competent technician—when he did the work—but added that he may be spending too much time being sociable.

Walter has always been easily distracted. It is hard for him to resist talking to his friends at work when they drop in and interrupt him. Often, he doesn't finish his own work but does favors for others. He is upset about his supervisor's comments and doesn't know what to do. He wants to do a good job and wants to keep his friends, too. One of his friends suggests he use a balance of consequences work sheet to help him decide what to do. The results are shown in Figure 10.3.

The balance of consequences work sheet can be expanded to include short- and long-term consequences, as shown in Figure 10.4. Walter could use this type of work sheet as a next step—for example, to highlight the difference between the positive and negative short-term effects of chatting with his friends (e.g., enjoyment) and the positive and negative long-term effects of turning his work in on time (e.g., a good performance appraisal).

Figure 10.3 Walter's Balance of Consequences Work Sheet

Action	Negative Consequences	Positive Consequences
Talking	Increased stress	Feels good
Doing favors	Poor performance appraisal	Feeling liked and accepted
Completing work	Feeling that I'm letting others down	Feeling more successful
	Feeling that I'm missing fun	Less stress
		Better performance appraisal

Figure 10.4 Short- and Long-Term Balance of Consequences Work Sheet

Specify the issue, question, or decision: _____

_____

List the short-term positives: List the short-term negatives:

_____   _____

_____   _____

_____   _____

_____   _____

List the long-term positives: List the long-term negatives:

_____   _____

_____   _____

_____   _____

_____   _____

Sequential Organizer, or Time Line

A time line can help you visualize which task to tackle first and which tasks are dependent on the ones that come before them. It helps you ensure that no important task is omitted. Before constructing your time line, you will have to brainstorm all the tasks or steps you must complete in order to solve the problem or make the decision. Refer to Chapter 6 for an example of a time line for a grant proposal.

Using Several Diagrams

You can use more than one diagram to help you solve a problem. As an example, Voncile was repeatedly having clashes with a coworker and couldn't understand why. She decided to use a fishbone to help her figure out what could be causing the trouble (see Figure 10.5). Maybe her coworker just didn't like her. Maybe the coworker thought Voncile was in competition with her. Possibly, Voncile had inadvertently insulted her in some way. Or the coworker could be having problems at home that had nothing to do with Voncile.

She reviewed the possible causes as displayed on the diagram and was able to generate four possible solutions. Now she had to decide which one of these approaches would work the best for her. She used a pro/con chart to help her think it through (see Figure 10.6).

After carefully deliberating and examining her charts, Voncile decided to invite her coworker out for dinner.

Figure 10.5 Voncile's Fishbone Diagram

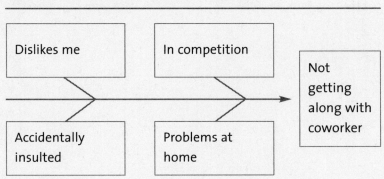

Figure 10.6 **Voncile's Pro/Con Chart**

Possible Solutions	Pro	Con
Ignore the problem	Avoid conflict and embarrassment	Problem persists or gets worse
Talk to coworker	Work toward a solution or resolution	Possible conflict or anger
Talk to coworker's boss	Get it off my chest Get help or advice	Could backfire and make boss and/or coworker angry at me
Invite coworker out for dinner	Make the first move and act graciously Attempt to deal with the problem	Expensive Coworker could rebuff me or laugh at me

These charts and diagrams can also help you with goal setting, which we talk about next.

Setting Goals

Many people with ADD have low aspirations, despite their potential. They are afraid to raise their sights any higher because of negative experiences that they had in school or on the job. They are afraid to set goals, even if they hate their jobs or are dissatisfied with their lives. When they do try to set goals, they don't use a systematic approach, and so, they often fail.

Using a systematic approach can help you set realistic goals and help you attain those goals. Goal setting is a necessity, not a nicety. Setting goals can bring hope and motivation into your life. Research indicates that merely setting some goals can enhance your performance. Goal setting can also help reduce some of your stress and increase your confidence and self-esteem. Above all, goal setting can help you live up to your potential.

A Systematic Approach to Goal Setting

Whether you are trying to set a goal or are working toward attaining a goal, you will use the same tools and skills that you used for making decisions. First, though, comes the process of developing the goal. If you invest the time to carefully develop it, you can work toward achieving it in a more determined and focused manner.

When developing your goal, describe it as specifically as possible. For example, don't write, "I want to focus my attention better." A more specific statement would be, "I want to be able to focus and maintain my attention when I work on the new project at work [name of project], which starts next week and is due at the end of the month." Include where the activity will take place, when you want to attain the goal, and who or what else might be involved.

If you can, describe the goal in positive terms. It is more motivating to increase a positive than decrease a negative. For example, "I will spend two hours each month de-cluttering my room" is preferable to "I will stop being a slob."

Your goal needs to be realistic and attainable, so it needs to involve conditions that you control. Distinguish between a dream and reality. Start with a small goal. Small goals are more do-able. You can (and should) divide a large goal into smaller ones. Also, be sure to give yourself enough time to achieve your goal, and take into account your pattern of strengths and weaknesses.

When trying to determine if a goal is attainable, consider any problems or barriers that interfered with your goals at other times. Do these same problems or barriers still exist? Can you overcome them this time? Identify some activities that will help you attain your goal. Seeking advice from someone you respect and trust is often advantageous.

Make sure you select a goal that is relatively easy to attain. This will increase your motivation to stay focused on the goal and to make progress toward its completion. Write out your goal, to imprint it in your memory, and describe why it is important to you. Then post it prominently at home or at work so that you can remind yourself of your goal at least once a week.

A well-developed goal will include the steps and tasks needed to attain it, as well as a time line for completion. Maintaining your motivation will be much easier if you use a systematic approach.

Goal-Setting Checklist

The goal-setting checklist is similar to the previous checklists in this chapter. This list includes self-talk and visualization, since they are fundamental to maintaining motivation.

Set the goal:
❑ Is it specific, attainable, and important?
❑ Does it take into account your pattern of weaknesses and strengths?
❑ Can you break the goal down into smaller, intermediary goals?
❑ Are there related goals?
❑ Do you need to gather information before you set the goal?
❑ Write the goal out clearly, and be specific.

Make a plan:
❑ Visualize the goal.
❑ Visualize the steps and tasks you will need to complete to achieve your goal.
❑ List the steps and tasks.
❑ Decide on a starting date.
❑ Set a deadline.
❑ Develop a time line.
❑ Are there people whose help you need?

Maintain motivation:
❑ Check off steps and tasks as you complete them.
❑ Use encouraging self-talk.
❑ Visualize the goal and how good you will feel when you attain it.

❑ Plan rewards for yourself.

❑ Ask friends and family to cheer you on.

❑ Review your goal once a week.

Monitor and adjust:

❑ Ask yourself: "Am I making progress toward my goal? Should I make some changes?"

❑ Modify the goal, if necessary.

❑ Add or subtract tasks and steps, as needed.

❑ Locate additional information, as needed.

❑ Identify problems and trouble spots, and examine setbacks.

❑ Brainstorm possible remedies and their potential effects.

❑ Select the remedy with the best chance of success.

Common Problems Related to Goal Setting

Having too many goals can be discouraging and can dissipate your energy and undermine your motivation. Also avoid setting competing goals (e.g., family versus work). Check with your family about any goals that will have an impact on them. Always be sure to give yourself enough time to achieve your goals. Your newly acquired time-estimation skills (discussed in Chapter 6) will come in handy for this. Watch out for goals that are too difficult to attain at the present time. If these goals are important to you, postpone them to a later date — and set the date.

Types of Goals

You can set goals having to do with your performance on the job, upgrading your skills, going back to school, organizing your home, self-improvement, social relationships, and any other aspect of your life. Goals can be long term or short term. Long-term goals can take several years to accomplish. Short-term goals might take several weeks to a month to accomplish.

An example of a long-term goal is returning to school for retraining or certification. An example of a short-term goal is writing daily "to do" lists for a week. Short-term goals are much easier to accomplish than long-term ones, so if you are new to the goal-setting process, it is best to start with short-term ones. This book offers many examples of short-term goals from which you can choose. Remember: work on only one or two goals at a time.

You can also break down long-term goals into short-term goals. Using the long-term example in the preceding paragraph, a short-term goal might be taking one course toward certification. Always keep your long-term goals in mind when setting a short-term goal. Ask yourself: "Is my short-term goal compatible with one or more of my long-term goals? Does it lead in some way to one of my long-term goals?"

Being faced with problems and decisions is a normal and expected part of life. It is helpful to keep reminding yourself of that fact. When you are faced with a problem, tell yourself to take a deep breath and relax. Give yourself some time to think. Solving problems and making decisions effectively and efficiently can relieve you of a lot of stress and increase your sense of well-being.

This is also true of goal setting. We tend to put off setting goals as we concern ourselves with the problems of daily living. By using a systematic approach to problem solving and decision making, you gain more time for goal setting. Setting goals can increase your sense of control and your optimism about the future.

Remember, you do have choices. You can make real changes in your home or work life—even if you haven't been successful before. Now may be time for a new beginning.

Concluding Remarks

THE TOOLS AND STRATEGIES we have presented are not just for overcoming the problems posed by ADD; they are designed for a lifetime of use. The more you use them, the easier it gets so that eventually the process will become second nature to you. Remember: you can deploy these aids consciously whenever a need arises. Self-talk can see you through many a traffic jam. Visualizing can take you wherever you want to go. Routines can keep the lid on a life jam-packed with activity. Checklists can bring order out of chaos. "Stop!" can make the world stand still for a second while you take a deep breath and decide what to do next.

You may not be able to do it all alone, at first. You may need an ADD coach or therapist. However, applying the suggestions in this book can help you get on the right track; and if you fall off, get back on. You *can* have more control over your life, regardless of what life throws at you. Good luck!

Resources

Organizations

Attention Deficit Disorder Association (ADDA)
P.O. Box 543
Pottstown, PA 19464
484-945-2101
(fax) 610-970-7520
www.add.org

Attention Deficit Disorder Resources
223 Tacoma Avenue, Suite 100
Tacoma, WA 98402
253-759-5085
www.addresources.org

Children and Adults with Attention Deficit Disorder (CHADD)
8181 Professional Place, Suite 201
Landover, MD 20785
301-306-7070
(fax) 301-306-7090
www.chadd.org

Learning Disabilities Association of America (LDA)
4156 Library Road
Pittsburgh, PA 15234
412-341-1515
www.ldanatl.org

Coaching Resources

ADD Consults
www.addconsults.com

ADD Resources National ADHD Directory
253-759-5085
www.addresources.org

ADDA Coach Register
www.add.org

Managing Your Mind®
Coaching and Seminars
(phone and fax) 734-761-6498
www.managingyourmind.com
geri@managingyourmind.com

Nancy Ratey
www.nancyratey.com

Educational Materials and Other Resources

ADD Warehouse
800-233-9273
www.addwarehouse.com

ADDResource.com
www.addresources.org

Addvance.com
www.addvance.com
www.ncgiadd.org

LD Online
ldonline.org

National Resource Center on ADHD
800-233-4050
www.help4adhd.org

Newsletters, Magazines, and Informational Materials

ADDitude Magazine
42 W. Thirty-Eighth Street
New York, NY 10018
888-762-8475
www.additudemag.com

ADDult ADDvice Newsletter
223 Tacoma Avenue, Suite 100
Tacoma, WA 98402
www.addresources.org

The ADHD Report (by Russell Barkley, Ph.D.)
Guilford Press
800-365-7006
www.guilford.com

Attention! Magazine
Available with CHADD membership

Focus
Available with ADDA membership

Books and Audiotapes for Adults with ADD

Amen, D. G. *Healing ADD*. New York: Putnam, 2001.

Barkley, R. A. *ADHD and the Nature of Self-Control*. New York: Guilford Press, 1997.

Beck, A. *Cognitive Therapy and the Emotional Disorders*. New York: New American Library, 1976.

Biederman, J. *Economic Impact of ADHD*. Public News Release: American Medical Association, Sept. 9, 2004.

Davis, M., E. R. Eshelman, and M. McKay. *The Relaxation and Stress Reduction Workbook*. 5th ed. Oakland, CA: New Harbinger, 2002.

Ellis, A. *Reason and Emotion in Psychotherapy*. New York: Stuart, 1962.

Fellman, W. R. *Finding a Career That Works for You*. Plantation, FL: Specialty Press, 2000.

Goldman, D. *Emotional Intelligence*. New York: Bantam, 1995.

Goldstein, S. *Managing Attention and Learning Disorders in Late Adolescence and Adulthood: A Guide for Practitioners*. New York: John Wiley, 1997.

Hallowell, E. M., and J. J. Ratey. *Delivered from Distraction: Getting the Most Out of Life with Attention Deficit Disorder*. New York: Ballantine, 2005.

—— *Answers to Distraction*. New York: Pantheon, 1995.

—— *Driven to Distraction: Recognizing and Coping with Attention Deficit Disorder from Childhood Through Adulthood*. New York: Pantheon, 1994.

Hartman, T., E. M. Hallowell, and M. Popkin. *Attention Deficit Disorder: A Different Perception*. Grass Valley, CA: Underwood, 1997.

Hartman, T., and J. J. Ratey. *ADD Success Stories: A Guide to Fulfillment for Families with Attention Deficit Disorder—Maps, Guidebooks, and Travelogues for Hunters in This Farmer's World*. Grass Valley, CA: Underwood, 1995.

Kanfer, F. H., and A. P. Goldstein. *Helping People Change: A Textbook of Methods*. Elmsford, NY: Pergamon Press, 1980.

Kelly, K., and P. Ramundo. *You Mean I'm Not Lazy, Stupid, or Crazy?!* Cincinnati: Scribner, 1995.

Kolberg, J., and K. Nadeau. *ADD-Friendly Ways to Organize Your Life*. New York: Brunner-Routledge, 2002.

Luria, A. *The Role of Speech in the Regulation of Normal and Abnormal Behavior*. (Trans. by J. Tizard.) New York: Liveright, 1961.

Lyon, G. R., and N. S. Krasnegor, eds. *Attention, Memory, and Executive Function*. Baltimore: Brookes, 1996.

Mason, D. J., and M. L. Kohn. *The Memory Workbook: Breakthrough Techniques to Exercise Your Brain and Improve Your Memory*. Oakland, CA: New Harbinger, 2001.

Matlen, T. *Survival Tips for Women with ADHD: Beyond Piles, Palms, and Post-its*. Plantation, FL: Specialty Press, 2005.

Matlin, M. W. *Cognition*. 3rd ed. New York: Harcourt Brace, 2004.

McKay, M., N. Sonenberg, and P. Fanning. *Applied Relaxation*. (Audiotape.) Oakland, CA: New Harbinger Press, 1991.

Meichenbaum, D. *Cognitive Behavior Modification: An Integrative Approach*. New York: Plenum, 1977.

Morganstern, J. *Organizing from the Inside Out: The Foolproof System for Organizing Your Home, Your Office, and Your Life*. New York: Henry Holt, 1998.

Nadeau, K. G. *A Comprehensive Guide to Attention Deficit Disorder in Adults: Research, Diagnosis, and Treatment*. Levittown, PA: Brunner-Routledge, 1995.

Roberts, M. S. *Living Without Procrastination: How to Stop Postponing Your Life*. Oakland, CA: New Harbinger, 1996.

Shaywitz, S. E., and B. A. Shaywitz. "Unlocking Learning Disabilities: The Neurological Basis." In *Learning Disabilities: Lifelong Issues*, by S. Cramer and W. Ellis. Baltimore: Brookes, 1996.

Solden, S. *Journeys Through ADDulthood*. New York: Walker, 2002.

—— *Women with Attention Deficit Disorder*. (Audiotape.) Ann Arbor, MI: Frontier Audio, 1996. (Available at www.sarisolden.com.)

—— *Women with Attention Deficit Disorder*. Grass Valley, CA: Underwood, 1995.

Weiss, L. *Attention Deficit Disorder in Adults*. 3rd ed. Dallas: Taylor, 1997.

—— *ADD on the Job*. Dallas: Taylor, 1996.

West, R. L., and T. H. Crook. "Video Training of Imagery for Mature Adults." *Applied Cognitive Psychology* 6 (1992): 307–20.

Books and Audiotapes for Children with ADD

Barkley, R. A. *Taking Charge of ADHD: The Complete, Authoritative Guide for Parents.* New York: Gifford Press, 1995.

Carkhuff, R. R., and W. A. Anthony. *The Skills of Helping: An Introduction to Counseling Skills.* Amherst, MA: Human Resource Development Press, 1979.

Deshler, D. D., E. S. Ellis, and B. K. Lenz. *Teaching Adolescents with Learning Disabilities: Strategies and Methods.* 2nd ed. Denver: Love Publishing, 1996.

Deshler, D. D., and J. B. Schumaker. "Learning Strategies: An Instructional Alternative for Low-Achieving Students." *Exceptional Children* 52 (1986), 583–90.

Flick, G. L. *ADD/ADHD Behavior-Change Resource Kit: Ready-to-Use Strategies and Activities for Helping Children with Attention Deficit Disorder.* San Francisco: Jossey-Bass, 1998.

Greenbaum, J., and G. Markel. *Helping Adolescents with ADHD and Learning Disabilities: Ready-to-Use Tips, Techniques, and Checklists for School Success.* San Francisco: Jossey-Bass, 2001.

Harris, K. R. "Cognitive Behavior Modification: Application with Exceptional Students." *Focus on Exceptional Children* 15 (1982), 1–16.

Levine, M. *Ready or Not, Here Life Comes.* New York: Simon & Schuster, 2005.

—— *A Mind at a Time.* New York: Simon & Schuster, 2002.

—— *Educational Care: A System for Understanding and Helping Children with Learning Problems at Home and in School.* Cambridge, MA: Educators Publishing Service, 1994.

—— *All Kinds of Minds: A Young Student's Book About Learning Abilities and Learning Disorders.* Cambridge, MA: Educators Publishing Service, 1993.

Markel, G., and J. Greenbaum. *Performance Breakthroughs for Adolescents with Learning Disabilities or ADD: How to Help Students Suc-*

ceed in the Regular Education Classroom. Champaign, IL: Research Press, 1996.

Robins, A. L. *ADHD in Adolescents: Diagnosis and Treatment.* New York: Guilford Press, 1995.

Silver, L. B. *Attention-Deficit/Hyperactivity Disorder: A Clinical Guide to Diagnosis and Treatment for Health and Mental Health Professionals.* 2nd ed. Washington, DC: American Psychiatric Press, 1999.

Index

About the Authors

Judith Greenbaum, Ph.D., has worked with both adults and children with ADD, learning disabilities, and other special needs for the past thirty years. She received her Ph.D. in special education from the University of Michigan, where she taught teacher preparation courses in the Department of Special Education and was a research associate in the Programs for Educational Opportunity. In addition to coaching adults with ADD, she currently consults with schools and school districts in order to design educational programs for students with a variety of disabilities. She has written numerous articles on disability issues for *Washington Parent, Equity Coalition, Focus,* and Detroit's *Metro Parent* magazine, among others, and has conducted presentations and workshops for the Attention Deficit Disorder Association, Children and Adults with ADD, the ADDult Information Exchange Network, and the Learning Disabilities Association.

    Geraldine Markel, Ph.D., earned a doctorate in educational psychology and a master's degree in reading from the University of Michigan, where she served as faculty in Special Education and was director of High School and College Services at the Reading and Learning Skills Center. She has worked with secondary and postsecondary students who have learning disabilities, ADD, and emotional impairments. Currently, she is principal of Managing Your Mind® Coaching and Seminars. She speaks to professional and parent groups and serves as a work/life/school coach to adults and adolescents with ADD and learning disabilities. In addition, she presents work/life seminars at Fortune 500 corporations and is the coauthor of *Peterson's Parent's Guide to the SAT and ACT*.

Drs. Greenbaum and Markel are the coauthors of two books for teachers on ADHD and learning disabilities: *Helping Adolescents with ADHD and Learning Disabilities: Ready-to-Use Tips, Techniques, and Checklists for School Success* and *Performance Breakthroughs for Adolescents with Learning Disabilities or ADD*.